JOHN

Living Word BIBLE STUDIES

Joshua: All God's Good Promises
Nehemiah: Rebuilt and Rebuilding
Psalms, Volume 1: Songs along the Way
Psalms, Volume 2: Finding the Way to Prayer and Praise
Proverbs: The Ways of Wisdom
Ecclesiastes and Song of Songs: Wisdom's Searching and Finding
Isaiah: The Lord Saves
John: That You May Believe
Colossians and Philemon: Continue to Live in Him
1 & 2 Thessalonians: Living the Gospel to the End

John

That You May Believe

Kathleen Buswell Nielson

P&R

PUBLISHING

P.O. BOX 817 • PHILLIPSBURG • NEW JERSEY 08865-0817

Lay-flat edition released 2018

Printed in the United States of America

ISBN: 978-1-62995-585-8

Contents

Foreword

I sometimes think of John as the "inside-out and backwards gospel." I think of it as the "inside-out gospel" because it speaks to the heart—the heart of love that Jesus had for John as his "beloved disciple" and the heart of love that John invites us to have for Jesus. By touching our hearts, John's gospel has the power to change us from the inside out.

John is also the "backwards gospel" because of the way it opens and closes. Most writers—including many biblical authors—tell their readers why they are writing at the beginning. For example, Luke begins by telling his excellent friend Theophilus exactly why he wrote his gospel: "that you may have certainty concerning the things you have been taught" (Luke 1:4). But John waits until the end. It is not until the end that he tells us he has written these things "so that you may believe that Jesus is the Christ, the Son of God, and that by believing you may have life in his name" (John 20:21).

John's beginning is also backwards. Many writers—including some biblical authors—wait until the end of a book to summarize what they have said. For example, Mark keeps the full identity of Jesus Christ as the Son of God a secret until the end of his gospel. But John tells us what he wants us to know right from the start. His extraordinary prologue (John 1:1–18) states his thesis and opens up nearly all of the major themes in the gospel that follows.

These are all signs that John is unlike any other book that has ever been written. When people first explore the claims of Christ, they often hear recommendations to start with the gospel of John, and rightly so. This is the gospel where Jesus says "I am" this, and "I am" that, clarifying his true identity as the Son of God and Savior of the world. John is also the gospel in which Jesus performs seven "signs," or representative miracles, which demonstrate the full range of his saving power, even to the extent of raising Lazarus from the dead (John 11).

But this is not the climax of the gospel. Starting in chapter 13, John shows us the full extent of the love of Jesus, who went to the cross to die for our sins, before rising with life for the world. To read John by faith, therefore, is to know God's full gift of salvation in Jesus.

This study guide—which is the latest in Kathleen Nielson's exceptional series—is designed to take you deeper into John, deeper into the gospel, and deeper into Christ. It strikes an ideal balance between taking careful note of the details of the biblical text and capturing the broad sweep of John's narrative. It is faithful to Scripture. It is simple and clear in its explanations, thoughtful and provocative with its questions. Perhaps most helpfully of all, Dr. Nielson's sensibilities as a poet enable her to convey the full meaning and express the true beauty of John's many images (light and darkness, life and water, sheep and shepherd, etc.).

In short, this Bible study guide helps the gospel of John do what the Holy Spirit inspired it to do, which is to help you believe that Jesus is the Christ, and to have life in his name.

Philip Graham Ryken

A Personal Word from Kathleen

I began to write these Bible studies for the women in my own church group at College Church in Wheaton, Illinois. Under the leadership of Kent and Barbara Hughes, the church and that Bible study aimed to proclaim without fail the good news of the Word of God. What a joy, in that study and in many since, to see lives changed by the work of the Word, by the Spirit, for the glory of Christ.

In our Bible study group, we were looking for curriculum that would lead us into the meat of the Word and teach us how to take it in, whole Bible books at a time—the way they are given to us in Scripture. Finally, one of our leaders said, "Kathleen—how about if you just write it!" And so began one of the most joyful projects of my life: the writing of studies intended to help unleash the Word of God in people's lives. The writing began during a busy stage of my life—with three lively young boys and always a couple of college English courses to teach—but through that stage and every busy one since, a serious attention to studying the Bible has helped keep me focused, growing, and alive in the deepest ways. The Word of God will do that. If there's life and power in these studies, it is simply the life and power of the Scriptures to which they point. It is ultimately the life and power of the Savior who shines through all the Scriptures from beginning to end. How we need this life, in the midst of every busy and non-busy stage of our lives!

I don't think it is just the English teacher in me that leads me to this conclusion about our basic problem in Bible study these days: we've forgotten how to *read*! We're so used to fast food that we think we should be able to drive by the Scriptures periodically and pick up some easily digestible truths that someone else has wrapped up neatly for us. We've disowned that process of careful reading . . . observing the words . . . seeing the shape of a book and a passage . . . asking questions that take us into the text rather than away from it . . . digging into the Word and letting it speak! Through such a process, guided by the Spirit, the Word of God truly feeds our souls. Here's my prayer: that, by means of these studies, people would be further enabled to read the Scriptures profitably and thereby find life and nourishment in them, as we are each meant to do.

In all the busy stages of life and writing, I have been continually surrounded by pastors, teachers, and family who encourage and help me in this work, and for that I am grateful. The most wonderful guidance and encouragement come from my husband, Niel, whom I thank and for whom I thank God daily.

May God use these studies to lift up Christ and his Word, for his glory!

Introduction

When I think of the gospel of John, a picture comes to my mind—a picture of Jesus standing there saying, "Here I am. What are you looking for? *Here I am.*" Whether he's addressing a Jewish Pharisee or a Samaritan woman or a Roman official or a close companion, Jesus reveals *himself* as the divine answer to their need. "I am . . ." Jesus says repeatedly in this gospel.

John opens with a remarkably beautiful, mind-stretching statement of who Jesus is, followed by John the Baptist ushering Jesus directly on to the stage—where Jesus proceeds to tell us and show us just who he is. John clearly reveals Jesus' identity as the promised Christ, the Son of God, come to bring life to those who believe in his name (John 20:31). Jesus' identity and mission control the narrative, as he moves relentlessly toward the cross and resurrection and ascension. In these climactic events, the glory of who Jesus is and what he came to do shines. John wants his readers to believe in this Jesus, so that they will live and not die, now and forever.

We can't help but notice the differences between John and the Synoptic Gospels (Matthew, Mark, and Luke). In John we find no birth account, no actual baptism of Jesus or calling of the disciples, no temptation in the wilderness, no parables, no demons, no transfiguration, no institution of the Lord's Supper. The spotlight is a bit more focused. But only in the focused light of John do we find that first miracle, Nicodemus, the Samaritan woman, and many discourses—all wound into John's narrative to accomplish his aim of lighting up Jesus so that his reader will *believe*.

All the Gospels include Jesus' use of imagery to communicate his message. Only in John, however, do we receive such a gallery full of pictures through which Jesus reveals himself to the world. Light, wind, water, bread, shepherds, vines and branches—such images open up our minds and hearts to Christ himself, the Lord who made all the stuff of life and the one who comes in the flesh to redeem it. Through these images Jesus weds the most exalted spiritual truth to the most concrete reality; this is the beauty of the Word made flesh. This is what John wants us to see and believe. I pray that in your study of John you will take time to absorb the pictures, to meditate on them, so that the beautiful truth of Jesus will shine into all the concrete reality of your life, both now and in the very real days of eternity to come.

Do spend your study time focusing on the Word, passage by passage, as this study leads you to do. Some of the questions may seem easier or harder; they do reflect the complexity of this beautiful, many-layered gospel. That said, I encourage you to use the questions flexibly. If one seems difficult, don't let it halt you. There may be some questions, or parts of some, which you might want to wait on or come back to. The point is to spend the great majority of time taking in and musing on the Scripture itself. The Bible's living and active words are the words that change our hearts and lives, by the power of the Spirit.

This study assumes that the apostle John wrote this gospel. (Lesson 1 will treat John the writer in the biblical context.) There has been much critical discussion of authorship, which you can find summarized in several of the commentaries listed in the Notes. Most scholars date this gospel somewhere in the second half (and many in the last quarter) of the first century.

Many point to Ephesus as the place of writing, a center both of the church and of the Roman Empire. From such a point John's call rings out far and wide. He clearly speaks to Jews, continually showing how Jesus comes as the fulfillment of all their Old Testament law. And yet John speaks to every person of flesh and blood; he presents a God made flesh so that the world might believe and be saved. This call to believe, clearly summarized in John 20:31, comes not only to those who do not yet believe, but also to those who do—that they might *abide* in the one they believe in, bearing fruit until he comes again.

Whoever and wherever we are, John's gospel speaks to us. May it speak to you powerfully as you study and as the Spirit guides you to understand these words he led John to write. May you hear and believe Jesus' powerful "I am." May this Word live in your believing heart.

Initial Observations—Lesson 1

Lesson 1 (John 1:1–18)

Beginnings

Day One—Start by Reading!

The best way to begin study of a book is to read it! Whether you've read the gospel of John multiple times or never, give yourself this day to a rather quick read-through of chapters 1–10. Jot down initial thoughts and observations on the facing page.

Day Two—Read On!

Continue encountering this gospel in full, as you complete a quick read-through of chapters 11–21. Again, jot down initial thoughts and observations on the facing page.

Day Three—What and Who?

1. This is one book whose main idea we don't have to guess. Toward the end, the author clearly states his aim. Read John 20:30–31. Memorize verse 31, and

then write it out by memory. Underline words that stand out as key.

The gospel itself will open the meanings of these key words as we study. John's aim in writing will be continually evident, as he draws his reader to believe in who Jesus is and so find life in his name. For now, stop to say and pray again the words of John 20:31, asking that its aim will be accomplished in you and in others who read these Spirit-inspired words.

For reflection: Consider this not as an aim accomplished in a moment, but rather as an aim whose accomplishment begins and then continues through a lifetime into eternity.

2. In general, what aspects of this gospel did you notice in your initial reading that seem to reflect the purpose statement found in John 20:31?

3. Clear evidence has led many biblical scholars to conclude that it was the apostle John whom the Spirit led to establish this aim and develop a gospel around it, mentioning himself in this gospel only indirectly. If this is true (and so we shall assume in this study), what basic observations might you make about this author, from John 13:21–25; 19:26–27; 20:1–9; 21:20–24? See also Mark 1:16–20, 1 John 1:1–3, and Revelation 1:1–2.

4. Read or review the Introduction to this study, for other initial context.

Day Four—In the Beginning

As we open to the book's prologue, it is important to acknowledge that the whole book will unfold this prologue; at the start we will aim to understand it enough to be ready to understand it better and better.

1. This study's Introduction mentions some of the ways in which this gospel differs, particularly in its opening, from the other gospels. Read John 1:1–18, the book's prologue.

How would you describe John's method of introducing Jesus in this gospel? What is the general effect?

2. The prologue presents first and foremost the *Word* (Greek *logos*—which has many connotations, including the most basic one of expressing oneself through speech).

   a. Write down everything you can learn about this Word from John 1:1–5.

b. What connections might you note between John 1:1–5 and Genesis 1:1–5?

c. What understanding of the Word does the Old Testament bring to the New? Besides Genesis 1, see also Psalm 33:4, 6 and Psalm 107:17–20.

d. Considering the previous parts of this question, write down some thoughts on what it means that Jesus is the Word (as is finally clarified in John 1:14ff).

e. John 1:14 tells us that this Word was made flesh. How does expressing the incarnation in these words help communicate its awesome meaning?

3. In Colossians 1:15–17 and Hebrews 1:1–3a, what similar claims do you find concerning who Jesus is?

4. In John 1:4–9, the image of light emerges—an image that reappears in this book and throughout Scripture. Trace the light through these verses. What does this

image show us, and how does it reveal Jesus to us? How, too, might this light take us back to Genesis 1?

5. Let us recall John 20:31 at this point, which tells us that this gospel is written so that the readers will *believe* in *who Jesus is* and so find *life in his name*. In light of these key elements of John's theme, examine John 1:1–13.

   a. How do the elements of John's theme emerge right from the start?

b. In many ancient cultures, one's *name* was not just a title; it represented the essence of one's being or character. How does the prologue lay the foundation for true belief in Jesus' name?

c. How does John the Baptist in particular come on the stage bearing the message of John 20:31 (see vv. 6–8, 15)? What is John the Baptist's main role?

Day Five—Finishing with the Prologue

1. One can of course never "finish" with John's prologue; it is deep and, in many ways, beyond our understanding. Even in his profundity, however, John takes care to be as clear as possible. One way he does this throughout the book is by immediately clarifying his

positive statements with negative ones. For example, how do the negatives help clarify the positives in John 1:3, 5, 7–8?

2. The prologue tells what happened when this Word came into the world. How does John 1:9–10 make vivid both his coming and the response to his coming? How does John 1:11 make the tragedy of the response even more vivid?

3. In contrast, how does John 1:12–13 make vivid both the opposite response and then the result of that response? We shall see this result explained more fully throughout the gospel, but what do these verses tell us about the result?

4. The remaining verses of the prologue (John 1:14–18) stop to celebrate this Word's coming into the world and what it accomplished from the perspective of those who have received him and believed in his name. Consider what Jesus enabled believers to *see*.

   a. What Jesus lets us see had been glimpsed before. People saw the revelation of God's very being (his *glory*) in the Old Testament as well—but not fully. His glory was glimpsed in a tabernacle. That glimpse pointed ahead to Jesus who, according to John 1:14, became flesh and *dwelt* (literally "tabernacled" or "pitched his tent") among us. Read Exodus 25:8 and 40:34–38 and comment.

b. In John 1:14, 18, what kind of seeing is going on, and how does it depend completely on who Jesus is? *Note: The phrase "the only Son from the Father" implies not a created being (recall vv. 1–3), but a unique member of the Godhead. See the same "only" in verse 18 as well.*

5. Not only what we see but also what we *receive* through Jesus is crucial—and is also the completion of a process this God worked from the beginning, through the Old Testament, finally culminating in his Son. Read John 1:14, 16–17.

   a. What words repeatedly let us know the riches of what we receive through Christ? What do these words mean, and how are they exemplified in God's revelation of himself to us in Christ?

b. For background read Exodus 33:18–34:9. In what ways was the time of Moses and the law different from the time of Jesus' appearing, and in what ways was it the same?

6. Conclude by rereading John 1:1–18, stopping often to meditate on and thank God for his amazing plan of salvation, accomplished fully in his Son, the Word made flesh.

Notes for Lesson 1

Initial Observations—Lesson 2

Lesson 2 (John 1:19–51)

Seeing Christ

John's gospel, after the prologue, divides somewhat neatly into two parts (see Outline). The first part unfolds the identity and mission of this Word from heaven—rejected by many of his own, but offered in grace and truth to the world.

Day One—Getting Focused

1. We will stop regularly to ask how various passages develop the book's central aim, as we saw it in John 20:31 (see Lesson 1). First, renew your memorization of this verse. Then read this week's entire passage, John 1:19–51, looking in this initial overview for ways in which it unfolds that phrase expressing who Jesus is: "the Christ, the Son of God." Write your thoughts on the facing page.

2. How does the witness to Jesus' identity begin, and then get passed on and on, in John 1:19–51? (It will help to start with verse 33, recalling John 1:6.)

3. After the stretching context of the prologue, in these verses John moves quickly to the start of Jesus' active public ministry. Note all the references to time and sequence in John 1:19–2:1. What is the effect of this beginning?

4. Jesus begins his ministry in the northern part of Palestine, around the Sea of Galilee, not going south to Jerusalem until John 2:13. The first place mentioned (John 1:28) is not the Bethany near Jerusalem but somewhere "across the Jordan" (on the east side). Find the other places mentioned in John 1:28–2:13; consult a map to locate these cities. *Note: "Up" and "down" can imply topography*

rather than north and south; Jerusalem was at a higher elevation than Galilee. How does John's concrete focus on place and time affect the beginning of this gospel?

Day Two—John's Testimony, Part I (John 1:19–28)

Some initial background will help: "Jews" in John's writing can refer to all Jews or to a group of them, a group often hostile to Jesus and often comprised of Jewish leaders, such as the *Pharisees* (an influential group who stressed strict compliance with Old Testament law) or the *Sadducees* (not mentioned here, but who were the aristocrats of the Jews, powerful politically and economically). Priests and Levites were ministers and workers in the temple and would represent spiritual authority to the people.

1. The Jews as a people (including Jesus) were descendants of Abraham, living in the first century under Roman rule but anticipating a divinely promised deliverer. They were looking for the promised seed of Abraham, an eternal king in the line of King David. This king would be an *anointed one*—translated *Christ* (from the Greek) and *Messiah* (from the Hebrew). Comment on the ways in which the following Old Testament prophecies help explain the Jews' expectations in general—and this particular

interchange between John the Baptist and the Pharisees' messengers in John 1:19–27.

- Psalm 132:11–18; Isaiah 9:6–7

- Malachi 4:5–6; Luke 1:13–17

- Deuteronomy 18:15, 18

- Isaiah 40:1–5

- Matthew 11:7–15

2. When the Jewish authorities question John the Baptist's right to baptize (a practice at that time normally undergone by non-Jews converting to Judaism), he doesn't really explain himself. What is the thrust of his memorable response, in John 1:25–27?

   Indeed, how does John the Baptist fulfill the role established for him in the book's prologue by everything he says during this interchange (John 1:19–27)?

3. Look through the parallel passages in Matthew 3:1–6, Mark 1:1–4, and Luke 3:1–9. Clearly, the fulfillment of Isaiah 40 is central. How is John the Baptist "making straight the way of the Lord"?

Day Three—John's Testimony, Part II (John 1:29–34)

1. The very next day brings the opportunity for John the Baptist to clarify his witness concerning Jesus' identity. What do the ringing words of John 1:29 imply about Jesus, especially when we recall echoes of the larger biblical context of verses such as Exodus 12:1–13 and Isaiah 53:1–8?

2. Explain the logical twist of John 1:30 and how it might take us back to several different verses in the prologue.

3. John the Baptist had to have Jesus' true identity revealed to him before he could help reveal it to others. Through what steps did all this happen, in John 1:31–34? (See Matt. 3:13–17 for added context.)

4. How does this scene in John 1:32–34 let us glimpse "God in three persons, blessed Trinity"? What does the climactic witness in John 1:34 that Jesus is "the Son of God" mean, especially considering all that has come before it in this chapter?

5a. Examine in detail John's description of the Holy Spirit's role in relation to Jesus, according to John 1:32–33.

b. What context is added by Isaiah 11:1–2 and 61:1 (quoted by Jesus in Luke 4:18)?

c. In the context of the whole chapter so far, how would you explain the difference between John's baptism with water and Jesus' baptism with the Holy Spirit?

Day Four—More Witnesses (John 1:35–46)

1. What is John the Baptist's part in the activities of the next day, according to John 1:35–37? What is his part after verse 37? How might he have responded? How do you think he responded, and why? (After answering, peek ahead to John 3:25–30.)

2a. Read this first interchange between Jesus and Andrew and likely John himself in John 1:37–40. (The official call to discipleship in the other gospels probably came later, after this initial following.) What strikes you?

b. Consider John 1:41–42a, which shows the immediate outcome of this first interchange. What can we learn from the actions and words of this earliest Christian missionary activity?

3. John 1:42 brings Peter's first personal encounter with Jesus. How are Jesus' actions in this encounter full of hope for each individual who meets him? *Note: To name someone or something implied not only stating his character or essence but also exercising authority over him.*

4. Notice the similar pattern of activity in the next verses, John 1:43–46. Compare Andrew's and Philip's claims about Jesus in verses 41 and 45.

5. Philip identifies Jesus of Nazareth, the son of Joseph (identifications by which Jesus would have been known at that time), as the fulfillment of the Old Testament Scriptures (which included the Law and the Prophets). Nathanael apparently can't believe that the great Messiah could come from such a little town. How *might* Philip have responded, and what can we learn from his actual response in John 1:46?

Day Five—Jesus Sees and Lets Us See (John 1:47–51)

Jesus' encounter with Nathanael is mysterious and wonderful. We cannot know all the details. Some have conjectured, for example, that Nathanael earlier that day had been at home under his fig tree reading the Old Testament story of Jacob, a man of Israel in whom there was a lot of guile (see Gen. 27:35–36)! It is impossible to know, but it *is* helpful to review the Old Testament story that Jesus references in these verses. Begin this day of study by reading Genesis 28:10–17 along with John 1:47–51.

1. Review all the "seeing" and "looking" throughout the encounters of John 1:32–51. What do you see? In particular, what can we learn about Jesus' seeing, in John 1:47–48?

2. Nathanael responds with a ringing affirmation in John 1:49.

   a. Note these two titles for Jesus. How does the first title point to many such references throughout this first chapter?

b. We saw earlier the kingly expectations for the Messiah. Nathanael gets this second title right as well, even though, like the rest of Jesus' followers, he doesn't yet grasp the full meaning of Jesus' kingship. How do his affirmation (John 1:49) and the opening question of Jesus' response (John 1:50) let us glimpse progress toward John's aim stated in John 20:31?

3. John 1:51 is a huge pronouncement. We can tell that from Jesus' introductory phrase, which comes from the Hebrew for *Amen* and seems to say, "Listen! This is really true!" Commentators consistently note as well the change to plural in this verse's "you"—enlarging the promise to many more than just Nathanael. What is the picture of this verse, and how does it relate to Genesis 28:10–17? What awesome "gate of heaven" is being revealed?

4. The chapter's final title for Jesus is "Son of Man"—often chosen by Jesus to refer to himself. Read Daniel 7:13–14. How does this Old Testament passage describing Daniel's prophetic vision offer context for this title? How does this title combine helpfully with all the others throughout John 1?

5. Conclude by praying through the various names given to Jesus throughout this chapter, asking God to open your eyes more and more to see and believe in the full meaning of each of these names—so that, truly, "by believing you may have life in his name."

Notes for Lesson 2

Lesson 3 (John 2)

What This Christ Brings

Day One—Reading the Signs (John 2:1–11)

John 1 introduced us to the Messiah—the Christ, the Son of God. John 2 begins to show what this Messiah brings: first, glorious messianic promises fulfilled, and second, messianic warnings of judgment confirmed.

1. John 2 brings the first week of Jesus' public ministry to a climactic point with his first miracle, or *sign*. Read John 2:1–11, jotting down initial observations.

2. Read carefully in John 2:11 the summary comments on this first sign, and then reread John 20:30–31, John's statement of his central aim. Find and write down as many connections as possible between these verses. Finally, find the "Seven Signs" chart in the back, and fill in the first spaces.

3. What might it mean that in this first sign Jesus "manifested his glory" (John 2:11)? Connect this phrase with the prologue's introduction of Jesus (see John 1:3, 10, 14).

4. Having seen this first sign as part of the book's overarching plan, let's look at it in more detail. We don't know what was in Jesus' mother's mind in John 2:1–5, but we do know she brought to Jesus what was a terrible embarrassment for the host of this wedding feast. Jesus' response was actually quite tender and respectful, using the same expression—"Woman"—he used later for her during the crucifixion (John 19:26). To help clarify Jesus' reference to his "hour" in John 2:4, see the same word in John 7:30 and 17:1. With this background, muse and comment on this opening interchange between Jesus and his mother.

Day Two—A *Jewish* Wedding Feast

1. In this context of a Jewish gathering (note the jars "for the Jewish rites of purification" in v. 6), this miracle involving wine would have rich connotations.

   a. In the following passages, what part does wine play, and with what sorts of things is it associated? Look through Isaiah 25:6–9, Joel 2:21–29, and Amos 9:11–15.

b. How might the context of such rich Old Testament promises affect the people's views and expectations of this man who comes and turns well over 100 gallons of water into the finest wine?

2. Many have interpreted the stone water jars used for ceremonial washing as symbols of the traditional Jewish rites and rituals, which had become empty and lifeless for many of the Jews.

   a. What was God's view of those carrying out these rituals—for example, in Isaiah 1:12–18?

   b. Whether or not the symbolism of the jars is intended, in what ways does this wedding feast miracle show Jesus finally bringing life into the midst of a needy and waiting people? Recall again that end result promised in John 20:30–31.

3. As the Jews waited for their Messiah, they indeed lived in a God-ordained rhythm of religious rites and celebrations meant to point them to God and to his great redemptive plan. Jesus finally comes, enters that rhythm, and brings it to life—in himself. Note, for example, that after this intense first week, Jesus travels to Capernaum (by the Sea of Galilee) with his family and disciples, waiting there until *Passover* time to make the next move (John 2:12–13). In preparation for Day Three's study, review Exodus 12:1–28, and write your own summary of the significance of the yearly Passover celebration for the Jews. Then find the "Jewish Festivals" chart in the back, and fill in the first spaces.

Day Three—Zeal for Your House (John 2:13–17)

The Synoptic Gospels record a cleansing of the temple toward the end of Jesus' ministry. Many agree that the cleansing in John 2 is a separate, earlier event, with significantly different words spoken by the Christ as he enters the Jerusalem stage.

1. People streamed to Jerusalem for the Jewish feast days in order to worship and offer sacrifices at the temple as God had commanded. John 2:14 refers to the outer temple area, including the Court of the Gentiles, where non-Jews were welcome to come and pray. Evidently, salespeople (changing foreign money and selling animals for sacrifices) had invaded this area.

   a. Why would Jesus be especially concerned about this area of worship for the Gentiles? (Recall John 1:11–12.)

   b. Follow and visualize John's step-by-step account of Jesus in John 2:14–16. What observations can you make about Jesus from these verses?

2. John 2:17 interprets the previous verses as the disciples interpret the situation. Read Psalm 69:9, and look through the psalm to get a general feel for the nature and context and tone of it. In John 2:17, with its Old Testament quotation, what light is being shed on Jesus and his actions?

3. In his zeal, whom is Jesus reflecting? See, for example, Isaiah 9:7 and 26:11.

4. What are some aspects of the temple that would inspire such zeal? Before answering, read 1 Kings 8:6–30, 62–64.

5. Considering this background concerning the temple, along with the background of what we've learned of Jesus so far in this book, how is Jesus' very presence in

the temple an absolutely awesome event? How does the context of the Passover celebration, in which they were celebrating God's great deliverance of his people, make this event even more amazing and even ironic?

Day Four—Which Temple? (John 2:18–22)

1. Read John 2:18–22. How does this scene's conclusion echo the previous wedding scene's conclusion (John 2:11)? Read on to verse 23 and find similar echoes. Relate all this to the book's theme verses—John 20:30–31.

2. The "Jews" in this passage probably include leaders in the temple. These Jews, in contrast with the disciples, do not believe. How would you analyze their problem, in John 2:18–21? *Note: This was the temple Herod had been in the process of rebuilding already for forty-six years.*

3a. Summarize the interpretation of Jesus' words provided for us in John 2:21–22.

b. From John 2:18–22, what observations can you make concerning Jesus' death and concerning his resurrection from the dead? (See also John 10:17–18.)

c. Consider the appropriateness of Jesus' comparison. How would Jesus' death truly destroy the temple, as far as its role in the lives of God's people? How does Jesus in his death and resurrection actually become our temple? (See Rev. 21:22.)

4a. Consider John 2:11, 17, and 22 together. What means does God provide to help us see? What does this tell us about God and about how we should respond to him?

b. Which Scripture passages in reference to the resurrection might the disciples have remembered and believed later? Consider Psalm 16:10 and Isaiah 53:9–12 as possibilities.

Day Five—Seeing Jesus (John 2:23–25)

1. John 2:23 claims widespread belief in response to Jesus' signs and miracles, but what does John 2:24 imply about the belief of many? In what way can signs be misused and consequently unhelpful—as in John 2:18–20, 23?

2. Jesus' signs are meant to point beyond themselves to the identity of the one performing them. How does this chapter close with a focus on who Jesus is, in John 2:24–25? How is this description opposite to who we are?

3. As in the former scene with Nathanael, Jesus evidences his ability to know what is in man. In what ways does this divine view into the hearts of people lead you to respond? How should we respond to being known so deeply by the Lord Jesus Christ?

4. Look back through John 2 to review the ways Jesus is steadily revealing himself and beginning to show in these two crucial scenes what he as Messiah brings to this world. Try to summarize for yourself what he brings at the wedding and then in the temple. How is there great grace in all he brings?

Notes for Lesson 3

Lesson 4 (John 3)

Life in Christ . . . How?

We have been introduced to Jesus the Christ by the apostle John's inspired writing, by John the Baptist, and by Jesus' own words and signs. Now, in chapters 3–4, come three personal encounters that, along with John's commentary, unfold the meaning of this "life in his name" offered to all who believe. First appears Nicodemus, who as a "ruler of the Jews" would have been a member of the Sanhedrin, the Jews' official ruling body.

Day One—Earthly vs. Heavenly Things (John 3:1–13)

1. Whether Nicodemus wanted secrecy or just a good quiet talk we don't know, but we can observe his initial attitude (John 3:1–2). What might logically have been the attitude of this well-educated, influential

Pharisee? What does appear to be his attitude . . . his starting point . . . his implied questions?

2. Nicodemus as a Pharisee would have been looking for a Messiah/King to come rescue the Jews and set up his kingdom (see Lesson 2, Day Two, question 1).

   a. What is Jesus saying about those expectations (John 3:3), and why does Nicodemus not understand what Jesus says (John 3:4)?

   b. What pattern similar to that of John 3:3–4 do you find in John 2:19–20? What is the consistent problem of Jesus' hearers?

3. Examine Jesus' answer as he repeats his claim with added emphasis and detail in John 3:5. Many have discussed the possible meanings of this verse and especially this "water." It is helpful first to connect these words with a number of Old Testament promises, especially one that Nicodemus surely would have known: Ezekiel 36:22–26. How do both water and Spirit work together here to point toward the fulfillment of God's redemptive work in his people? What things does Ezekiel say the water and the Spirit accomplish?

4. A Pharisee like Nicodemus would have put a great deal of trust in external things, like physical parentage and obedience to the law. Jesus is talking about a whole different category of things.

    a. With what reasoning and with what picture does Jesus try to open Nicodemus' eyes to this other realm, in John 3:6–8? *Note: One Greek word—and one Hebrew word as well—can mean either "wind" or "spirit."*

b. How do Jesus' words to Nicodemus about birth take us back to John 1:12–13, clarifying those opening words even further?

c. Why is "birth" a great image to communicate what is needed in people like Nicodemus—and in all of us?

5. When Nicodemus doesn't understand (John 3:9), how (and why) does Jesus challenge him, in John 3:10–12?

Note 1: Jesus' use of "we," plural, in verse 11, is not explained; he may be speaking as a representative of the Trinity, whose full presence in heaven he is recalling with these words.

Note 2: In John 3:7, 11–12, Jesus switches from singular to plural in his use of "you." Although he's just speaking to Nicodemus, the truth of John 1:11 may be in his mind.

6. The main way Jesus answers Nicodemus' confusion is to talk about himself. Before reaching the climactic verse, observe carefully John 3:11–13 and write down everything you can learn about Jesus from these verses. How do you respond?

Day Two—Believe or Not (John 3:14–21)

1. Jesus offers one climactic picture of the spiritual transformation Nicodemus needs. Again, it is a picture this Old Testament expert would know.

   a. Read Numbers 21:4–9 and John 3:14–15, making note of all the connections you see.

   b. For added context, read John 12:32–34 and 2 Corinthians 5:21, and comment on this lifting up of the Son of Man, so that sin-bitten men might live.

2. How does this passage (John 3:1–15) clearly show that being given spiritual life is the work of God, not something we can do ourselves?

3. How does John 3:1–15 also clearly show that human beings are called to respond in a certain way to the work of God in order to receive that life? How does this take us right back to the book's theme verse (John 20:31)?

4. The call to believe in him in order to have eternal life (John 3:15) leads directly into the next section, which many believe is the apostle John's commentary on the

previous scene. We noted earlier that John excels at clarifying truth by pointing out what it is and what it's *not*! Spend the rest of this day reading and analyzing John 3:16–21, listing all the *opposites* you can find in these verses—many of which use the word *not*!

Day Three—For God So Loved (John 3:16–21)

1. Look through your list of opposites from Day Two, question 4. Why would John want to include so much negativity in his description of salvation?

2. John 3:16 is simple and powerful, as it tells God's redemptive plan. Read the following notes and consider these questions: What parts of this verse did Nicodemus especially need to understand? What parts do you need increasingly to understand?

   - *so*—implies "in this way" rather than "so much"
   - *world*—The Greek *kosmos* has many shades of meaning: sometimes the created universe; sometimes people and systems opposed to Christ; sometimes all or many human beings; sometimes humanity in general, often with the added sense of fallenness or opposition to God (as here)
   - *only*—unique (uniquely representing the Father)
   - *perish*—the opposite of eternal life, that is, eternal deathly torment
   - *eternal life*—pictured throughout Scripture as not just never-ending life, but life in the joy and communion of the eternal God's holy presence.

3. John 3:1–8 emphasized the work of the Spirit; John 3:9–15 highlighted the Son. What various aspects and activities of God the Father emerge in John 3:16–21?

4. Again, the human response is crucial. Which words tell us what people we're talking about in John 3:16–21? Which words tell us what these people are to do?

5a. Consider the light and darkness in John 3:19–21. What is it about the light that people without Christ fear? Have you ever known or seen that fear at work? Explain briefly.

b. Why can we as believers come to the light without fear? See John 3:21.

6. Nicodemus seems to be holding on to the darkness even while seeking the light. Peek ahead to find evidence that more than just the physical wind was blowing during that nighttime interview. Read John 7:45–52 and 19:38–42. How does the work of God in this man's life give you hope?

Day Four—A Faithful Witness (John 3:22–30)

Read the context in John 3:22–24. John is telling of a period not covered in the Synoptic Gospels (see Mark 1:14). Read also John 4:1–2. The disciples' baptizing was probably a continuation of John the Baptist's baptism of repentance, in preparation for receiving Jesus.

1. Note the problem that arises in John 3:25–26. Before reading John's response, recall the words about him in John 1:6–8 and his own words in John 1:19–28. What is your diagnosis of this problem?

2. John the Baptist deals with the problem gently but clearly. What are the implications of his statement in John 3:27 for *himself*? For *Jesus*? For *us*?

3. Not only does John affirm his previous words in John 3:28, but he also goes on to help these disciples by means of a picture.

   a. How does this picture in John 3:29 effectively communicate John's point? What tone and what emotion do you find here?

b. What added context is provided by Old Testament passages such as Isaiah 62:1–5 and Hosea 2:16–20?

4. John the Baptist disappears from this gospel after his ringing words in John 3:30. In what ways can the truth of this verse increasingly affect you, your prayers, your motivations, and your ambitions?

Day Five—Rescue Sent from Heaven (John 3:31–36)

Again, many think the following section is the apostle John's commentary. In any case, this little paragraph beautifully concludes John the Baptist's witness to Jesus the Christ and draws our thoughts back to who Jesus is.

1. What is the main point of John 3:31, and in what ways is that point emphasized through these three statements?

2. This section does what John the writer often does: spirals back and recaptures ideas already presented. How does John 3:32 echo John 3:11? How does John 3:32–33 echo John 1:11–12? What is the effect, as you read?

3. Setting one's seal was to imprint one's mark of ownership or authenticity. According to John 3:33, to what are we personally committing ourselves when we receive Jesus for who he says he is? According to John 3:34–35, in what ways does Jesus connect us with the Father? After answering these two questions, take a moment to reflect on the amazing route God has opened up to himself—

the awesome gate to heaven God has provided through his own Son.

4. John 3:36 concludes, not surprisingly, with one more statement of opposites.

   a. What is the opposite of believing, in this verse, and how is this appropriate?

   b. How is the opposite of eternal life explained vividly and almost joltingly? (Recall the contrasts in John 3:16, 18, which this contrast seems to bring to a climax.)

c. How do these contrasts shed light on John's central aim for his book (John 20:31)?

d. How do these contrasts impact your thinking about the gospel and the ways in which you show and share it?

Notes for Lesson 4

Lesson 5 (John 4)

Christ Comes to the World

The interviews continue, as John shows us how truly Jesus meant the "whoever" of John 3:16. First came Nicodemus the Pharisee. Now come a Samaritan woman and an official of the Roman government.

Day One—Contexts (John 4:1–9)

John 4:1 implies that Jesus knows it is not yet time for confrontation with the Pharisees. His journey back north (John 4:3) is clearly directed by a sense of mission, as John 4:4 might suggest as well. Samaria lay right between Judea in the South and Galilee in the North. In the days of Israel's kings, Samaria had been part of the Northern Kingdom, which was conquered by Assyria in 722 B.C. Many of the people were taken captive, and Assyria brought in foreigners to inhabit Samaria—foreigners who intermarried with the remaining Jews. The result was a people of mixed race and mixed-up religion, combining aspects of Judaism with other religions. Samaritans, for example, worshiped not in

Jerusalem but on Mt. Gerizim, not far from this woman's town of Sychar. Jews of Jesus' day would not associate with Samaritans, considering them corrupt and unclean. Many Jews would travel *around* Samaria, not *through* it.

1. All this history, even going back to Jacob and Joseph (John 4:5–6), reminds us of the crucial Old Testament context in which Jesus makes his appearance. Take a moment to page through the previous lessons and notice the many Old Testament references that have been so intimately connected to John's gospel. What would you say if somebody asked you, "Why is the Old Testament important to the gospel of John?"

2. Consider not just the historical but the physical context here as well. The "sixth hour" was noon—the hot part of the day, when most people would not be out drawing water. Read John 4:6, 8, and picture the scene. What strikes you?

3. Now picture this Samaritan woman walking up by herself, carrying her water jar. Jesus' first words to her are more shocking than we can imagine. If Jews did not associate with Samaritans, Jewish men *absolutely* did not associate (especially publicly) with female Samaritans.

    a. What aspects of Jesus might his request in John 4:7 reveal?

    b. What aspects of Jesus have we seen previously that might affect our perception of this scene as it opens?

4. What aspects of the woman might her response in John 4:9 reveal?

5. For the remainder of this day's study, read John 4:7–26 and write down initial observations and thoughts.

Day Two—Living Water (John 4:10–20)

1. Although the woman immediately focuses on the "living water" (which in the Greek can also mean *fresh spring water*), Jesus' words in John 4:10 ask her to focus on what? What familiar pattern of conversation do you recognize in John 4:10–11? Of what previous interchanges does it remind you?

2. After the woman adds some almost taunting words concerning Jesus' identity (John 4:12), Jesus describes the water he can give.

a. First, read carefully John 4:13–14. What do these pictures communicate about this water?

b. What further light is shed by John 7:37–39?

c. What have we seen so far, concerning Jesus and the Holy Spirit, in John 1:32–33 and 3:34?

d. To Nicodemus, Jesus spoke of receiving life as being "born of water and the Spirit" (John 3:5). How wonderful: believing in Jesus happens through the Holy Spirit and involves receiving the Holy Spirit. We shall read more about the Spirit in John, but for now, look back to the Old Testament to see how the following passages pave the way for Jesus' announcement of such water: Isaiah 12:3; 44:1–3; 55:1–3; Jeremiah 2:12–13; Ezekiel 47:1–12 (just catch a glimpse of Ezekiel's prophetic vision!).

3. In response to the woman's request in John 4:15, why do you think Jesus brings up all these painful personal details in John 4:16–18? And then why do you think she responds as she does in John 4:19–20?

4. Write your thoughts on this picture of water in relation to your own experience, considering questions such as the following: In what ways have you known this thirst to be filled with such water? Why is it crucial to acknowledge first that the Lord God sees all the deepest needs and darkness of your heart? In what ways does this water keep us from being thirsty again?

What does it mean that this spring of water is welling up to eternal life in us?

Day Three—Spiritual Progress (John 4:21–42)

1. The woman asks about external worship, but Jesus responds by addressing spiritual worship—that realm of things Nicodemus couldn't seem to get his head around. *Note: The word* spirit *in John 4:21–24 refers not to the Holy Spirit, but to the invisible spiritual realm.*

    a. What truths is Jesus affirming in verses 21–24? With what questions might these truths leave the woman?

b. Recall this word *truth* back in John 1:14, 17–18. Picture Jesus standing there saying these things to the Samaritan woman. How might John 4:25 indicate that she is getting Jesus' message?

2. What an amazing declaration in John 4:26! No other open declaration of his identity is given by Jesus again until his trial. Why do you think Jesus speaks so openly here?

3. The results of this interview multiply quickly and beautifully.

   a. In John 4:27–30 and 39–42, what noticeable factors are involved in bringing people to *believe*? Which of these factors have you seen at work in leading people to believe?

b. What names for Jesus in these verses let us know that these people are truly believing? How do we see John 3:16–17 in action in these verses?

4. In what way does Jesus similarly teach the disciples to look beyond the visible realm in John 4:31–34? How might his comments here relate to the interview just concluded?

5. Examine this picture of the harvest, set right in the middle of a story about the harvest happening!

   a. Read John 4:35–38. How does Jesus use this picture to urge his disciples to follow him?

b. How might Jesus be referring to the role of John the Baptist in this picture?

c. What are the implications of this picture, set in the middle of this story, for you as a believer today?

DAY FOUR—BELIEVING THE WORD (JOHN 4:43–54)

As these opening chapters come full circle, Jesus arrives back at the place of his first sign (John 4:43–46; John 2:1) and performs his second sign here in his home territory where he is not yet honored (John 4:44). Like the first, this sign is offered to reveal who he is so that people might believe.

1. First came a Jewish Pharisee, then a Samaritan woman, and now comes an official of the Roman government. Read John 4:46–54, fill in the next spaces on the

"Seven Signs" chart, and jot down initial observations or thoughts.

2. In John 4:47–48, Jesus responds to the official's request with "you" (plural). Whom might he be addressing here, and what is his point?

3. When the official persists, Jesus offers him a kind of dilemma. See John 4:49–50.

   a. How might the official have responded differently?

b. How does his actual response address Jesus' previous comment about signs?

c. How does the official's response challenge you?

4. Relish the joy of the remainder of the story, in John 4:51–54.

   a. What different outcomes do we see, and how do they differ from one another?

b. How might we better balance such different outcomes in our own prayers and praises?

5. The nature and timing of this second sign highlight what aspects of Jesus' power? How might this take us back to the book's opening words and the very nature of Jesus himself?

Day Five—From the Beginning, Jesus

1. Through the Samaritans and the government official, we are glimpsing the coming of Jesus as a light to all the nations of the world. The Jews were chosen to bear the seed of the Savior through generations of preparation for his coming. But from the beginning God meant to bless all peoples through the witness of his people, and ultimately through his Son. How is this God-ordained

worldwide blessing evident in the following representative passages:

- Genesis 12:1–3

- Isaiah 2:1–4

- Isaiah 49:5–6 (spoken by the Servant, a pre-figuring of Christ, as the New Testament makes clear—see also Acts 13:44–48)

- John 1:11–13

2. Think back through the three encounters—with Nicodemus, the Samaritan woman, and the official. Why does Nicodemus seem to struggle most to understand and receive the truth? We know that only the Spirit brings a person to life, but what various factors can we see God using, factors that help people have and maintain open hearts toward Jesus and the life he offers?

3. These encounters, encased in the two signs, have helped clarify just who Jesus the Christ is and what sort of life he brings. The focus is all on Jesus. How good for us to participate in that focus! What stands out to you in the portrait of Jesus so far in John? Say aloud that theme verse (John 20:31), and consider the ways in which this verse is unfolding as this gospel begins to develop.

Notes for Lesson 5

Lesson 6 (John 5)

Witnesses to the Christ

Now that the identity and mission of Christ have begun to unfold, the opposition begins to unfold dramatically. The next section of John begins again with another sign—back in Jerusalem, during another Jewish feast (the only unidentified one in John). Fill in the "Jewish Festivals" chart—even though the significance of this feast does not seem to be crucial for the passage.

Day One—A Healing and More (John 5:1–17)

1. Read first through the whole of chapter 5, writing down initial observations and thoughts. From your first reading, how would you describe the shape or basic outline of this chapter? Take time to fill in the "Seven Signs" chart.

2. Read carefully the description of the healing (John 5:1–9a) and then the related events (John 5:9b–17).

   a. What impressions do you get of this invalid?

   b. If this is not a story about his faith, what is this story about?

   c. What appears to be Jesus' main concern with him, and how is this consistent with Jesus' previous personal encounters?

3. This scene begins a whole string of confrontations, in which Jewish leaders use Sabbath rules as ammunition. The Old Testament actually says nothing about carrying bedrolls on the Sabbath! Jewish traditions had built up all sorts of detailed, extra rules that had come to be considered law. For background, read Exodus 20:8–11 and Deuteronomy 5:12–15. What is the focus of the Old Testament commands concerning the Sabbath?

Day Two—Jesus and His Father (John 5:17–24)

1. Jesus will talk about the Sabbath in other contexts, but here he makes one point. What is that point, in John 5:17, and what do you think of the Jews' response in John 5:18? *Note: Jews evidently concurred that God is always at work in the sense that he moment by moment sustains and directs the universe he created.*

2. Jesus has just shown and then stated his divine power. What follows in the rest of the chapter is an amazing discourse on that subject—specifically on his relationship to God his Father. How does John 5:19 (introduced by that emphatic "Truly, truly") show both the equality of the Son with the Father, and yet also the Son's subordination to the Father? Write down some thoughts on why both are so crucial.

3. Muse on that first sentence of John 5:20. How does this enlarge our understanding of the Trinity (God in three persons)? How does this enlarge our understanding of Jesus' experience of life on this earth?

4a. In John 5:20b–21, what is the basic assumption—as is clear, for example, in Deuteronomy 32:39 and 1 Samuel 2:6?

b. To what future events might Jesus be referring?

c. How might *life* here have more than one level of meaning?

5a. What is the underlying assumption in John 5:22—as is clear, for example, in Psalm 96:10–13?

b. Who is both the subject and the primary actor (John 5:22), and what is his aim in this astounding act of giving (John 5:23)? How does all this contribute to the point of this scene in John?

6. John 5:24 is a powerful capstone to this little section and a great summary of the book's message. How do the various phrases work together to deepen and confirm the meaning? For example, hearing Jesus' word is equated with what? What kind of *life* is unfolded here, as far as its alternative, its starting point, and its quality and duration?

Day Three—Now and Then Implications (John 5:25–29)

1. Read John 5:25–29. What themes from the previous section (see Day Two) are developed here specifically in relation to the day of resurrection and judgment? *Note: Scripture teaches that the resurrection and judgment will occur at Jesus' second coming, the climax of this present period inaugurated by Jesus' first coming.*

2. According to John 5:25, 28–29, by what means will Jesus' resurrecting power be executed? How have we already seen glimpses of this power in previous passages of John?

3. Muse for a moment on John 5:26. What does it mean that Jesus (through the Father) has "life in himself"? (Recall John 1:1–4.) Many commentators contrast this life with our "derived" life as created human beings. What is the difference, and what difference does it make in how you think of your own life?

4. Consider the aspects of Jesus' judgment revealed in John 5:27–30.

   a. How does Jesus' identity as the "Son of Man" relate to his authority to execute judgment? (Recall Dan. 7:13–14, as well as the truly human nature implied by this name.)

b. John 5:29 does not teach salvation through our good works, although it teaches judgment of our works. Why can we say that? See John 3:16 and Ephesians 2:8–9, but go on to Ephesians 2:10 to help explain. What is the first "work" we are called to do, according to John 6:28–29?

c. How does John 5:30 give us confidence concerning Jesus' judgment?

5. How amazing to see Jesus looking ahead to the cross and way beyond, as if he sees it all laid out right in front of him! What can we learn from this eternal perspective, even as we sometimes struggle to see the next day or week?

Day Four—Witnesses (John 5:30–47)

1. How might you summarize the main point Jesus is making in John 5:30–38?

2. John's gospel, as we have seen, is full of witnesses to the identity of Jesus. In what ways does Jesus use John the Baptist's witness, in John 5:32–36? (See also Ps. 132:13–18.)

3. Jesus' greatest witness, of course, is his Father, according to John 5:36–39.

    a. In what ways has that witness come?

b. In what ways has God's witness been rejected? (By contrast, consider how some have faithfully received God's consistent witness—for example, Moses in Exodus 3:1–4 and 33:11, the psalmist of Psalm 119:11, John the Baptist, and the Roman government official.)

4. The final verses of this chapter emphasize the written word, the revelation through which God has chosen to offer his witness through generations. How would you summarize Jesus' main point about Scripture, in John 5:38–40, 45–47?

5. If someone asked you what it means that Moses (who wrote the first five books of the Bible) wrote about Jesus, how would you answer? How have we seen the truth of this in our study of John so far?

Day Five—Implications

1. In this whole passage, Jesus has explained how he receives glory from his Father, not from people (see John 5:41).

   a. In John 5:41–44, how are the people about whom he's speaking different from him?

b. What might be some implications of these verses for you and for the church today? From what directions do we all tend to seek glory and honor?

2. In this last passage (John 5:30–47), there are huge implications concerning our study of Scripture. What are some of the dangers—and the blessings—of studying the Bible that emerge in these words of Jesus?

3. Think back to (and repeat by memory) that guiding verse, John 20:31. What crucial elements of that verse do you find woven into John 5—and woven together with the concept of *the Word*? As you conclude this lesson, what would you pray concerning words and the Word?

Notes for Lesson 6

Lesson 7 (John 6)

Christ the Bread

John 6 brings the fourth and fifth signs, further clarification of Jesus' identity and mission, more marked antagonism from those who will not believe, and a huge, wonderful blessing for those of us who will.

Day One—Physical Food (John 6:1–15)

1. Read the context of John 6:1–4 and fill in the "Jewish Festivals" chart. For this second Passover of his public ministry Jesus does not go to Jerusalem, but he does build his actions and words on the meaning of this celebration. Review the details of Passover in Lesson 3, Day Two, question 3.

2. The actual sign in John 6:5–15 offers the foundation on which the whole chapter will build. First, fill in the "Seven Signs" chart. Then examine the various

perspectives and expectations of the participants in this scene: Jesus, the crowd, and the disciples.

3. Picture this scene, with its five thousand men—along with women and children (see Matt. 14:21). What details of the narrative stand out to you in John 6:5–13?

4. Jesus makes increasingly clear what he means by saying Moses wrote about him (John 5:46). Parallels abound—and Jesus will develop them—between this miracle and Moses' story of the Exodus and the wilderness wanderings. Read through Exodus 16; what parallels do you find?

5. The people understand that Jesus is the prophet of whom Moses wrote (see John 6:14, and recall Deut. 18:15, 18). However, they want to force him to do what they think that prophet should do for them. In what ways do we all share and witness that same desire?

Day Two—Bread from Heaven (John 6:16–31)

What a full day had passed! But the events at the end of it were just as dramatic. Read John 6:16–21 and the corresponding account in Mark 6:45–52. Again, fill in the chart of "Seven Signs."

1. What aspects of Jesus does this amazing little incident reveal? *Note: John 6:20 is the first of many announcements of what can literally be translated "I am." For all the original hearers, the words may not have echoed with God's revelation of himself to Moses in Exodus 3:14 or through the prophets (see Isa. 43). Certainly, though, especially as they accumulate in this gospel, these words echo more and more with Jesus' clear announcement of his divinity.*

2. What various words do John and Mark use to communicate the disciples' emotions during this scene? In what ways can you identify with the disciples' experience?

3. In John 6:1, they had crossed to the east side of the Sea of Galilee. Now (John 6:16) they have sailed (or walked!) back to the west side, to Capernaum. Follow the chasings around the north end of this sea, in John 6:22–25. Then read on.

   a. When the people catch up with him, consider Jesus' words in John 6:26–27. What familiar contrast is Jesus making here? Where have we seen it before?

   b. What are the key elements in the process of getting the right kind of food (John 6:27)?

4. How do the comments of the people in John 6:28, 30–31 show that they don't understand this process?

5. Jesus' words in John 6:29 offer to correct their understanding. How does this verse help correct our many human tendencies to misunderstand salvation?

Day Three—Jesus and Bread (John 6:32–51)

This whole interchange between Jesus and the Jews (John 6:25–59) turns on Jesus' use of food, specifically bread, as a metaphor for the life offered in himself. To use a metaphor is to name or describe one thing in terms of a second, in order to express the truth of the first through the second. For example, we see the truth of the Spirit in the wind blowing, or we understand the death and resurrection of Jesus in the temple's being destroyed and raised up in three days. Again and again, Jesus shows us spiritual truth through concrete pictures. God in the flesh has a unique ability to create the most powerful metaphors.

1. Jesus acted out his metaphor in the miraculous feeding; now he is explaining his metaphor in John 6:32–35. His answer includes his first direct "I am" statement, the first of seven such beautiful metaphors by which Jesus comes into this world and explains himself through everything in it. Make your first entry in the chart of "I Am" statements. Then imagine that someone asks you why Jesus calls himself "the bread of life." How would you answer?

2. We might wonder how these people could have seen Jesus and not believed (John 6:36). However, in John 6:37–40, how are we told repeatedly on whom this believing depends? (On whose *will* does belief depend?) How do these verses point us toward the far-reaching implications of this truth? After answering, stop to ponder the comfort and security these truths can offer.

3. Read John 6:41–46, which confirms both their unbelief and the point Jesus has just made about belief. (See also John 6:60–61.) How do these Jews resemble their forefathers? (Recall Ex. 16, and see Num. 14:26–30.)

4. The quotation in John 6:45 would bring to the Jews' minds a whole flood of verses from the mid-section of Isaiah, which is all about the suffering Servant to come. Look through Isaiah 53, for example, to recall the context and to see it being fulfilled by Jesus. Isaiah 54 is the joyful response to Isaiah 53, celebrating what God will do through this one despised and rejected by men. Look through Isaiah 54, finding Jesus' quotation (Isa. 54:13) in its original context. Now, for what reasons might Jesus use this quotation in his own context (see John 6:41–46)?

5. In John 6:47–51, how does Jesus both rehearse his metaphorical point and develop it further—in a very difficult way?

6. To confirm your last answer, read John 6:52–59. What repeated words stand out?

Day Four—A Hard Saying (John 6:52–60)

1. How do those repeated words in John 6:52–59 seem deliberately to make Jesus' message a hard one to take in?

a. The elements of flesh being eaten and blood being spilt tell us that a death is involved in the life Jesus is promising here. How were those very elements crucial to the Passover celebration the Jews were celebrating?

b. Recall John the Baptist's first words at Jesus' approach in John 1:29. How are those words being fleshed out here? (See also 1 Cor. 5:7.)

2. How does the metaphor work, in John 6:52–59? If the bread is Jesus (and his very flesh *sacrificed*), then to eat this bread would be to . . . ? Put another way, if physical life comes from eating physical bread, then eternal life comes from . . . ? Before answering:

a. Compare John 6:54 to 6:40.

b. Read John 6:47, 48.

c. Refer also to John 3:14–16, 6:29, and 20:31.

3. Grasping the metaphor here leads us to conclude that Jesus is saying more than that we need to participate in the Lord's Supper (the full meaning of which developed later, in the early church). However, when we do rightly celebrate the sacrament of the Lord's Supper, how do we affirm the true meaning of what Jesus is teaching here? (Refer to 1 Cor. 11:23–26.)

4. Jesus often repeats his main message, but he is always unfolding its meaning. For example, not only does Jesus promise life that will burst out in final resurrection, but he also describes that life in the present tense, in John 6:56. According to what we've seen of this metaphor, what is this kind of continual feeding? What is this *abiding* Jesus speaks of? Can you testify to the meaning of this from your own experience?

5. According to John 6:60, 66–67, not just the Jews in general but even many of the disciples found Jesus' teaching hard. What were the reasons they found it hard? How might people today—or might we—find Jesus' teaching hard for some of the same reasons?

Day Five—Words of Life (John 6:60–71)

Seeing the people's "offense" at his teaching of the bread come from heaven, Jesus retorts by wondering how much greater will be the offense when that bread is taken back up into heaven—referring to his ascension and perhaps all the passion events that immediately precede it (John 6:62). It is that spiritual realm to which they are blind.

1. How does Jesus point the way into that realm, in John 6:63? What are the keys? (See also John 3:5–6.)

2. How does John 6:63 explain why these people didn't get Jesus' teaching about the bread? How does it lead us to receive this teaching? (See also Deut. 8:3.)

3. John 6:64–65 reminds us of what, concerning Jesus? (Is John perhaps reminding us of who Jesus is, from

the beginning—as in John 1:1?) How does Jesus' awareness of his divine mission from beginning to end help us understand each incident, each chapter, more fully?

4. Spend some moments meditating on Jesus' question and Peter's powerful response in John 6:67–69. What does Peter *believe*, and how does he help clarify the meaning of that word? Peter does not yet understand it all, but this picture of him face to face with Jesus, trusting in his words and trusting in him, is beautiful and challenging, is it not? *Note: This new title for the Christ, the "Holy One of God," perhaps connects to the Old Testament title—especially Isaiah's—of God as the Holy One of Israel. It affirms that Jesus is from God and set apart for the Messiah's divinely appointed task.*

5. But this section does not end with Peter's words. How must Jesus' words in those final two verses have affected Peter? How do they affect the flow of the narrative, as John is shaping it?

6. Conclude by saying out loud the words of John 20:31 and considering how everything in this chapter (and this book!) has been focused toward that end.

Notes for Lesson 7

Lesson 8 (John 7–8)

Confrontations with Christ

John's chapters would all reward weeks and months of study! But we will move a bit more quickly in this lesson, grasping the crucial themes and seeing the flow of John's narrative. We are deep into the unfolding revelation of Jesus' identity and mission—as well as the growing antagonism toward him among the Jews. Jesus comes to offer life to all who *will* receive him, but he first displays that offer before his own who will *not* receive him, for he comes to fulfill all God's promises to them.

Day One—God's Time (John 7:1–10)

1. The Feast of Booths (or Tabernacles) is the crucial context for these next chapters. Fill in the "Jewish Festivals" chart, and then read the background (Lev. 23:33–36, 39–43; Deut. 16:13–15) to note the practices and purposes of this huge, week-long celebration in Jerusalem.

2. John 7:1–5 shows antagonism not just in Jerusalem but also at home in Galilee. What sort of worldly wisdom do Jesus' brothers (probably sons of Joseph and Mary) offer him?

3. In John 7:6–9, Jesus repeatedly uses the word *time*. *Note: this is different from "hour," which often refers specifically to his being lifted up on the cross. The Greek* kairos *here usually indicates a time larger than passing moments—more like a season.*

   a. According to what kind of time is Jesus living? (Refer also to John 5:19–20; 6:38.)

   b. What might Jesus mean that his brothers' time "is always here"?

c. In what ways might you be like these brothers? How can we live more and more according to Jesus' time?

4. Jesus does go to Jerusalem, at just the right time and in the right way (John 7:10). Chapters 7 and 8 are made up of his teachings there, his interchanges with the people, and their increasingly antagonistic responses. In preparation for a closer study of all these words spoken back and forth, read through John 7–8, making note of initial observations and thoughts.

5. Your text may note that the earliest manuscripts do not include John 7:53–8:11 and that this passage is not generally considered to be legitimately part of John's inspired gospel. We will not deal with it further. However, this incident may well have happened and in fact

does not contradict other scriptural content. Examine the way the text follows naturally from John 7:52 into John 8:12. But take time to note as well, in this passage, the aims both of the Pharisees and of Jesus in dealing with this woman.

Day Two—Listening and Learning (passages from John 7–8)

For each of the following questions, examine John 7:11–36, 40–52, and 8:13–30. The goal is to listen in carefully on these interchanges, in order to grasp the heart of the interaction between Jesus and his listeners.

1. In what ways does Jesus continually communicate who he is, especially in relation to his Father?

2. Examine the various responses of the people to Jesus.

   a. In what ways are some drawn to him?

b. At what points do they just misunderstand who he is or what he says? Why do they misunderstand?

c. At what points do they reject him? How and why does this take place?

d. Record any other observations about the people's response to Jesus.

e. What personal experience have you had with any of these responses?

3. What insights does Jesus offer into the people who confront him? What basic judgments are scattered throughout these verses—judgments that reveal the people's true need?

4. Which of these verses make clear the sovereignly planned events to come, Jesus' death and resurrection and ascension? How do these verses affect the whole narrative?

5. What have we missed? As you examine these verses, what other observations come to mind? How would you summarize these interchanges at this point?

Day Three—Water and Light (John 7:37–39; 8:12)

In two instances at this Feast of Booths Jesus takes an important part of the celebration and shows how it is a picture of the spiritual life he brings.

First, *water*: Every day of this Feast of Booths the High Priest led a procession of priests from the temple to the Pool of Siloam (outside the city's southern gate—there was no water source in Jerusalem), where they filled a golden vessel with water. This water they carried back and poured on the altar with great pomp and ceremony. In this way they celebrated God's provision of water from the rock during the Israelites' desert wanderings (Ex. 17:1–7), and water that had nurtured and still nurtured the crops in the Promised Land where they lived.

Second, *light*: The lighting of the oil lamps in the temple's Court of the Women was a festive part of each evening during this Feast, with singing of psalms and great celebration, as light shone out over the city from the high point of the temple. Through this they celebrated God's provision of light in the pillar that guided the Israelites with cloud by day and fire by night through the wilderness wanderings (Ex. 13:21–22).

1. Jesus has used the picture of water already in a private conversation; now he applies it publicly, on the climactic day of this feast. Read John 7:37–39 and consider four brief questions: What does this water picture? How is one eligible to receive it? How do we get it? What's the water like? *Note: We have seen the Spirit at work in and through Jesus, and we know the Spirit has been at work from the beginning. Here John refers to the pouring out of the Spirit that will happen at Pentecost after Christ's*

death, resurrection, and ascension. Jesus will speak more about this before John is finished.

2. Jesus refers to "Scripture" here not in terms of one verse but as a whole flow of Old Testament promises that he has come to fulfill. Review the verses noted in Lesson 5, Day Two, question 2d. See also 1 Corinthians 10:1–4.

3. Consider Jesus' second "I am" statement, in John 8:12 (fill in the appropriate chart). How do these words take us back to the book's prologue?

4. How could we ever trace the huge flow of verses relating to light, all of which culminate in Jesus? For example, read Genesis 1:1–3; Psalm 27:1; Psalm 119:105 (connect this to Jesus the Word); Isaiah 9:2–7; and Isaiah 49:6

one more time. This is a large subject, but take a few moments to read, reflect, and comment on what this darkness and light mean to our world.

5. We must look ahead! According to Revelation 22:1–5, how will we know water and light in that new Jerusalem of the new heaven and earth?

DAY FOUR—WORDS OF TRUTH (JOHN 8:31–47)

1. The remainder of John 8 might be said to hang on Jesus' statement in John 8:31–32, where the "if" clause (concerning his word) is basic. In John 8:31–47, trace all the statements concerning Jesus' word, asking the question:

"What is the difference between believers and unbelievers, in relation to Jesus' word?"

2. Jesus' listeners hear just that last part—concerning freedom from slavery.

   a. According to John 8:32–33, what familiar sort of misunderstanding is taking place?

   b. According to John 8:33–41, what do these Jews not know about themselves, and what is the main substance of their delusion?

c. In what ways is this delusion a common one, even today?

3. To attack the Jews' delusions, what contrasts does Jesus set up in John 8:34–47? These verses are complex, but aim to get at the way Jesus keeps relentlessly separating truth from falsehood, light from darkness.

4. What is true about truth, according to this passage (John 8:31–47)? What observations can we make about the kind of truth Jesus offers?

5. Which of these observations about truth might not be very popular in the world today, and why?

Day Five—The Great "I Am" (John 8:48–59)

1. In this concluding passage, Jesus not only reiterates his relationship to his Father God, but he also makes his climactic statement about the result of keeping his word (John 8:49–51). What things are at stake here, according to Jesus' words?

2. Analyze the Jews' several responses to Jesus throughout this concluding passage. What are they perceiving? What are they missing?

3. In his second statement, Jesus is claiming divine knowledge—not only of his Father, but of their father Abraham—perhaps referring in general to Abraham's joyful faith in God's promises, which he is saying were all about him. But how is that final claim, in John 8:58, the most amazing? What is Jesus' claim here? Look again to Exodus 3:13–14, as well as to the many uses throughout Isaiah 43 of these words "I am."

4. This climactic claim brings a climactic rejection—and the disappearance of Jesus, who is not ready for the climactic confrontation. Look back through these two chapters. What has been Jesus' aim in coming to this Feast of Booths? His aim, of course, could be stated in a variety of ways; what different ways do you think best capture what he has been about here?

5. Review and consider the book's central aim, in John 20:31. How would you say these chapters fit into that larger aim? In what way have these chapters helped you see Jesus more clearly and believe in him more deeply as the Christ, the Son of God?

Notes for Lesson 8

Lesson 9 (John 9)

Christ the Light

John 8 ended with the Jews' decisive and violent rejection of their Messiah. Jesus disappears from sight, remains in Jerusalem, and then reappears as he sets his sight on one needy man.

Day One—Getting the Shape

Read through John 9, jotting down initial observations. Construct an outline that captures this chapter's shape. Write down a statement of this chapter's main subject. (There is not one right outline or summary!) Finally, fill in the "Seven Signs" chart.

Day Two—Getting the Real Story (John 9:1–7)

1. Having read John 9, how would you explain its connections to the previous chapter (specifically John 8:12)?

2. In John 9:1–3 Jesus enlarges his disciples' perspectives on the causes and effects at work within human experience.

   a. All suffering in general results from the sin and brokenness of this fallen world. How can specific suffering also result from specific sin? (See, for example, Num. 12:1–10 and 1 Cor. 11:29–30.)

b. What other cause and effect, however, does Jesus reveal to be at work in this case?

c. How might Jesus' teaching here lead us to deal differently with our own suffering or the suffering of others?

3. According to John 9:4–5, Jesus sees this encounter as an opportunity given by his Father during his short time of

earthly work. What is the purpose of this work? Connect these verses to John 1:9–18.

4. How does the Old Testament context illumine the purpose of this chapter's particular work? See, for example, Isaiah 35:1–6; 42:1–7.

5. We cannot explain with certainty all the details of this healing. (Why mud and saliva?) However, in what ways might some of the details help reveal who Jesus is (John 9:1–7)?

Day Three—Post-Miracle Interviews (John 9:8–34)

1. The first post-miracle interview might be titled "The Basic Facts" (John 9:8–12). Why do you think the local people find it so hard to grasp these facts? What strikes you about the way the man himself tells the facts?

2. Let's title the second interview "Pharisees Groping in the Dark" (John 9:13–17).

    a. The Pharisees (also called "Jews," meaning Jewish leaders) have appeared before in this gospel; how might previous scenes help interpret this one?

b. Imagine the healed man watching all this. What would he see? What does he see concerning Jesus at this point?

3. Then comes "Parents Afraid to See" (John 9:18–23). What is going on in these parents? What are they giving up—and for what? In what ways might you be acquainted with this kind of struggle?

4. Once they can no longer refute the miracle, "The Jews Strike Back"—both at Jesus and at this man who testi-

fies of him (John 9:24–34). Analyze the nature of the Jewish leaders' debate methods here.

5. The healed man is only a beginning theologian, but he is a wise one. In what various ways does he refute the Jews' arguments against Jesus (John 9:24–34)?

Day Four—Seeing and Believing (John 9:1–38)

1. Find all the references to "birth" and being "born" in John 9:1–34. Why do you think this is emphasized so strongly? In answering, consider questions such as the following: How does the fact that the man was blind from

birth reveal the power of this sign? How are the Jews both wrong and right, in verse 34? (See John 1:11–13.)

2. How have we seen this man develop, in John 9:1–34? Why do you think Jesus left him alone after the healing, until this particular point?

3. But now he is ready. Examine carefully the simple interchange in John 9:35–38.

   a. What a beautiful example of belief occurring before our eyes. How would you describe Jesus in these verses?

b. How would you describe the man? What necessary parts of "believing" do we find in this scene?

c. How do Jesus' words, "You have seen him" appropriately sum up the story at this point?

d. How is the book's purpose statement (John 20:30–31) beautifully confirmed here?

4. But the incident does not end here. The large themes of blindness and sight, darkness and light (with both the negative and positive sides, as we have come to expect)

will be effectively concluded. Read John 9:39–41, in preparation for the final day of study, jotting down your initial thoughts and observations.

Day Five—Light Embraced or Rejected (John 9:39–41)

1. Jesus speaks in John 9:39 of judgment that separates which two categories? How would you explain these pictures? (Which is the blind man, and which is the Pharisees?)

2. Even though he comes not to condemn but to save, how does Jesus in his coming necessarily bring judgment? How does preaching the gospel inevitably bring both

salvation and judgment (both sight and blindness)? See also John 3:17–19 and Isaiah 6:8–10.

3. Why does Jesus condemn the Pharisees for saying, "We see"? How is blindness their judgment?

4. In what ways have you been tempted (or are you tempted) to be like the Pharisees in this story? In what ways must the church aim not to be like these Pharisees?

5. John 9 has shown Jesus coming to save *whom*? How does it happen? Write down your thoughts and prayers in response.

Notes for Lesson 9

Initial Observations—Lesson 10

Lesson 10 (John 10)

Christ the Shepherd

The next picture through which Jesus reveals himself communicates even more personally who he is and what he has come to do for those who believe in him. We are coming to the end of the scenes where Jesus will teach publicly about the life he offers in himself.

Day One—Shepherds and the Shepherd

To begin, read through John 10 and Ezekiel 34. What seems to be the relationship between these two chapters? How have we seen similar relationships in previous chapters? Write down your initial observations and thoughts.

Day Two—Figures of Speech (John 10:1–6)

1. Note, in John 10:1–2, the two contrasting figures.
   a. How does Ezekiel 34:1–10 shed light on this thief/robber figure?

b. How does Ezekiel 34:11–16 shed light on this shepherd?

2. In what ways did John 9 prepare us for these figures? How does John 10 logically follow John 9?

3. The picture is of a sheep pen holding numerous flocks, into which a shepherd would come and collect his flock by his personal call, which only his sheep would recognize. What aspects of the shepherd and his sheep seem to be emphasized in this initial picture (see John 10:2–5)? What details stand out?

4. John 10:6 tells us that the Jewish leaders (perhaps the same crowd from the previous chapter—see v. 21) don't get this "figure of speech." Recall some of Jesus' words to them in previous chapters to suggest reasons for their lack of understanding.

5. In this initial picture (John 10:1–6) what comforts you? What warns you or instructs you? How might these words make you pray?

Day Three—The Door and the Shepherd (John 10:7–18)

1. Jesus takes the picture's images and develops them in various ways. First, in John 10:7–10, examine the ways in which Jesus explores this image of the *door* (or the *gate*) in relation to himself. (Fill in the chart of "I Am" statements.)

a. What do you see, as you picture Jesus as the door or gate for sheep? Consider various implications of this image.

b. If Nathanael is listening here (recall Gen. 28:10–17 and John 1:51), what related picture might come to his mind?

2. Compare and contrast the rewards of those who walk through the door of the false shepherds with the rewards of those who walk through the door provided from heaven. Use both Psalm 23 and John 10:7–10 in your comments.

3. Think back over the miracles and images so far in this book. What details especially picture not just life, but over-the-top, abundant life? What is the nature of this life? Consider how John 10:10 might be misunderstood, and why.

4. A shepherd in Jesus' time would sometimes lie down across the sheep pen's opening at night, making a door with his body. Perhaps this helps us transition from the *door* to the *shepherd*, the chapter's central image. Note that both "I Am" statements here are given twice (John 10:7–18).
   a. Fill in the chart again, making only one entry for each statement.
   b. In each case, after saying it the first time Jesus develops the negative contrast, and after the second time he develops the positive implications. First, then, how is what the good shepherd does (John 10:11) specifically contrasted with what his opposite does (John 10:12–13)?

5. Now let's consider the positive implications, and they are many (enough to flow into the next day's study). In John 10:11–18, how many times does Jesus mention what the good shepherd does? Each time he says it how does he expand its meaning just a little more in the comments around it?

Day Four—The Authoritative Shepherd (John 10:16–30)

1. Look one more time at the conclusion of this discourse about the shepherd.

   a. In John 10:14–18, how do Jesus' divine knowledge and power clearly emerge?

   b. As Jesus here anticipates his death, how would you sum up his perspective on the cross and the resurrection? Consider also Peter's more theological version in 1 Peter 2:24–25.

c. How might you sum up John 10:16?

2. How might you describe the response of the Jews in John 10:19–21, in terms of the healing-of-the-blind-man story, or in terms of the shepherd imagery (see John 10:26)?

3. John 10:22–23 brings us to another feast, one established by the Jews to commemorate their overthrow of Syrian oppression: Judas Maccabaeus in 164 B.C. had led the Jews in reclaiming their temple, where the wicked Antiochus Epiphanes had set up a pagan altar. Here they are at the Feast of Dedication (Hanukkah, which was in December, when the protection of Solomon's porch would have been welcome), speaking with the very one to whom all their worship should be dedicated. Fill in the "Jewish Festivals" chart.

   a. Contrast the Jews' question and Jesus' answer here (John 10:24–26) with the parallel scenes in John 4:25–26 and John 9:35–37. What was different in those other two scenes?

   b. What do you think Jesus means by saying he has already told them who he is (John 10:25)?

4. The rest of Jesus' answer describes the security Jesus gives his sheep—as if he's saying to these false shepherds, "You can't have them; they are mine." In John 10:27–30, what are the various aspects of this security, and why can we fully rest in it?

5. Note the parallel pictures of hands. What happens as you picture these images, one verse after the next, in John 10:28–30? How do you respond?

Day Five—A Stopping Point (John 10:31–42)

1. It is Jesus' statement, "I and the Father are one," that provokes another attempt to stone him (John 10:30–31). Stop and consider that claim, and the similar one in John 10:38. (Recall John 1:1–2, and review John 5:18–23.) We cannot fully grasp just what it means that Jesus is the Son

of God, but what aspects of this relationship are clearly crucial for us to remember and believe?

2. In John 10:32–38, Jesus supports and develops this claim concerning his Father.

   a. How does Jesus use his *works* in this argument? See John 10:32, 37–38, and recall John 10:25.

   b. How do the Jews miss Jesus' point about his works, in John 10:33? What do they understand and not understand?

c. Read John 10:34–36 and Psalm 82, in which the Lord addresses "gods" and "sons of the Most High" who are ruling unjustly. The psalm is difficult, but Jesus seems to be using a purely logical argument from Scripture in order to refute these Jews who stake their arguments on the letter of the law. How does Jesus (even as he argues that it is technically not blasphemy for him to call himself the Son of God) clarify his unique identity as the Son of God?

3. John 10:40–42 brings a turning point in the book, as Jesus' public ministry ends and he returns full circle to the place where John baptized. Recall the purpose of John the Baptist in the book's prologue. In what ways is that purpose validated in these final verses of John 10?

4. John tells us that the end result he's after for the readers of his book is *life* in Jesus' name. Look back through

John 10:1–30, and find all the references to *life*. How do these references together help explain that *life* promised in John 20:31?

5. Before we move ahead to see Jesus bringing this life even more openly, a further (selective) review will be helpful, to recall what we've seen of this life. Turn back to John 1:4; 3:16; 4:13–14; 5:39–40; 6:35; and 8:12. We so often think of life as an abstract concept. How does Jesus make us think about *life*?

Notes for Lesson 10

Lesson 11 (John 11)

Christ the Resurrection and the Life

John 11 brings the climactic miracle, one which displays the life Jesus offers in himself—and one which propels him forward to the cross, where his glory will shine out.

Day One—Going for Glory (John 11:1–16)

1. John 11:1–2 sets the context, identifying first the problem and then the place: the Bethany of Mary and Martha (see also John 11:18)—as opposed to the Bethany of John 1:28. John identifies this Mary as the one who anointed him—even before he gets to that story in John 12. With the context set, consider the urgent message that precipitates the action in John 11:3. How might the sisters have phrased this message

differently? What do you observe about the way they did phrase it?

2. What crucial perspectives on this story can we gain from the various phrases of Jesus' response in John 11:4? How do John 1:14 and 2:11 shed added light?

3. Read the next section, John 11:5–16.

   a. How might the opening sentence seem confusing in light of the next one? Why is this simple sentence so important and beautiful?

b. How does the goal stated in verse 4 shape Jesus' plan of action through verse 15?

c. How do John 8:12 and 9:4–5 shed light on John 11:7–10? How is Jesus answering the disciples' protest that it is dangerous to head back toward Jerusalem?

4. Jesus is surrounded by disciples who don't yet see the light clearly. Consider the examples of dim understanding in John 11:1–16. How does Jesus handle this dimness? Be sure to notice Thomas in verse 16. What does he seem to understand or not understand?

5. For Jesus everything was about shining the light of God's glory—ultimately in the cross—so that people might believe. How does this perspective challenge you as a character in the story God is directing?

DAY TWO—LIVING AND BELIEVING IN HIM (JOHN 11:17–27)

The story moves to Bethany, where a crowd of friends (many from Jerusalem) are still gathered to comfort Mary and Martha four days after their brother's burial.

1. In John 11:17–22 what various characteristics of Martha do you observe? How does the background story in Luke 10:38–42 give added perspective on this woman loved by Jesus? *Note: It is not clear just what Martha might have been asking in verse 22; it is perhaps more profitable to focus on what she is affirming.*

2. What is good about Martha's response in John 11:24 to Jesus' ringing promise in John 11:23? See also John 5:25–29 and 6:39–40.

3. We hear now with Martha the fifth of Jesus' "I am" statements, which ring with Jesus' divinity and reveal just what this God-made-flesh has brought down to us. Fill in the corresponding chart. In John 11:25–26, how is Jesus offering to Martha something more than the true theological assertion she has just made? What is Jesus showing Martha about *believing*? (Recall also John 3:16, 18.)

4. Examine the references to life and death in John 11:25–26. What two kinds of death is Jesus talking about? What kind of life? How and when does this life begin?

5. Martha understands the main point standing right in front of her, doesn't she! How does her response in John 11:27 affirm this?

6. Conclude this day's study by picturing Jesus standing there with this one woman, looking at her directly and asking her the question at the end of verse 26. How might this picture encourage you?

Day Three—Jesus Weeps with Us (John 11:28–42)

1. The third scene of this dramatic story focuses on the other sister. What can you observe about Mary from John 11:28–32? (See also Luke 10:39 and John 12:3.)

2. What precipitates Jesus' responses, and what do these responses reveal about him, in John 11:33–35? *Note: "Deeply moved" implies the strongest feelings, including anger.*

3. We can't move on from John 11:33–35 without responding ourselves to this glimpse into Jesus' heart. How do you respond?

4. How would you characterize the responses of the Jews (John 11:36–37)? What do they understand or not understand?

5. The fourth scene finally takes us to the tomb, where Jesus gives a command. What do you think of Martha's reaction to this command (vv. 38–39)?

6. Jesus' response, in John 11:40, does not reference a specific recorded statement to Martha, but what previous verses in this chapter does it recall? How does this response, as well as his prayer in John 11:41–42, provide an important reminder of what Jesus is aiming for here?

Day Four—"Lazarus, Come Out" (John 11:41–48)

1. Consider again the prayer of Jesus at Lazarus' tomb (John 11:41–42). What can we learn from this prayer about

Jesus' relationship and interaction with his Father? Why is this important just before the miracle is performed?

2. And now comes the sign itself (John 11:43–44). Take time to fill in the final spaces on the "Seven Signs" chart. How is the miracle performed, and with what previous passages in John might this connect?

3. Lazarus, who had been bound and wrapped for burial, perhaps staggered out of that tomb. What's he called in John 11:44, and why, do you think? Don't you wonder what he experienced? Why do you suppose we are not given his side of the story?

4. How does John 11:45 offer a wonderful conclusion to the story? Trace the various references to *believing* throughout this chapter; how does this get at what the whole story is about?

5. The conclusion, as always in John, is two-pronged; the "but" introducing John 11:46–48 should not surprise us. What do the Chief Priests and Pharisees of the Sanhedrin see? What do they fear? What do they desire most of all? How might we sometimes be tempted to think like them?

Day Five—Another Death and Resurrection (John 11:49–57)

1. Another "but" interrupts this final section! Read the words of Caiaphas the high priest in John 11:49–50 and John's commentary on those words in verses 51–53.

a. How would you characterize Caiaphas, just from this brief glimpse? Summarize the point he makes to these hand-wringing Jews.

b. Summarize the way John helps us understand a level of meaning deeper than what Caiaphas intended.

2. Substitutionary atonement (one dying on behalf of many) was taught by God to his people in the Old Testament. Read through Leviticus 16 to get the general picture of the sacrificial system God provided in order to picture the necessary atonement for our sins. Then read through Isaiah 53 to see the prophecy of the final atoning sacrifice of the promised Messiah. Jot down key phrases from your reading.

3. We have already seen the Old Testament prophecies of this salvation reaching not just Israel but all the nations—to which John alludes in John 11:52. (See Lesson 5, Day Five, question 1.) How would Caiaphas and his Sanhedrin have felt about this? What's the irony, then, in John 11:53 and in this whole passage?

4. Read the chapter's final verses (John 11:54–57), and fill in the final spaces on the "Jewish Festivals" chart. Note the purpose of the people's coming to Jerusalem, in verse 55. What will be required in order for this to happen, according to God's plan? Use some words from Isaiah 53 in your answer.

5. John 11, with the last sign, both culminates the book's first half and propels us forward into the second half, which will end with a much more momentous death and resurrection than that of Lazarus. In conclusion, think for a few moments on the glory of this Lord Jesus who is himself the resurrection and the life. How amazing to be called to believe, personally, in this Christ, the Son of God.

Notes for Lesson 11

Lesson 12 (John 12)

Christ Knows His Hour

In John 11, the Jewish leaders planned to put Jesus to death, and from that point on all the action moves inexorably toward the cross. As the third Passover of Jesus' public ministry approaches, the deliverance that Passover celebrates is about to be fully and finally accomplished by the Lamb of God who takes away the sin of the world.

Day One—Anointed for Burial (John 12:1–11)

1. Read John 12:1–8. In what ways does this passage point ahead to events about to happen?

2. John 12:7 is difficult, but at the least Jesus clearly connects Mary's anointing of him with the anointing of a dead body before burial. Whether or not Mary herself understood this, what was Mary showing by her action here? What words would you use to describe Mary? Refer also to the parallel scenes in Matthew 26:6–13 and Mark 14:3–9. (Yes, Mary probably anointed Jesus' head *and* feet.)

   Note #1: Washing feet was the lowliest servants' job.

   Note #2: Women customarily kept their hair bound in public.

   Note #3: Three hundred denarii represented a whole year's wages for a common worker.

3. In what ways do Mary and Judas offer a stark contrast in this scene? What is the main point of difference?

4. Analyze the escalating tension in John 12:9–11. What different things are growing? What is the logic of the chief priests at this point? How is their logic flawed?

5. Read on to the next day's passage to find the same motivation of the crowd and the same desperation of the Jewish leaders (John 12:12–19). How do the sovereign time and place and nature of that last sign emerge even more clearly, as we see it bearing fruit? How do Jesus' words in John 11:4 begin to grow in meaning?

Day Two—The First Palm Sunday (John 12:12–19)

1. First, read John 12:12–13 along with its Old Testament context, Psalm 118:25–26. Psalm 118 is part of a group of psalms rehearsing the deliverance of the Exodus, sung regularly at Passover, blessing and welcoming those coming

up to Jerusalem to celebrate this feast. What phrase do the people add to the Old Testament quotation here? What are its implications? *Note: Palms were part of many Jewish feasts and celebrations, considered a kind of national emblem.*

2. Other gospels give more details, but what basic things does John want to communicate in John 12:14–15? See also Zechariah 9:9; what aspects of this deliverer are emphasized in that prophetic verse (aspects that perhaps this crowd was not ready to celebrate)?

3. John 12:16 might remind us of John 2:22. After Jesus was *glorified* (that is, after his death and resurrection), the salvation brought by this Christ would become clear. The whole book (and the whole of Scripture!) has been

leading up to this glory. How is everyone in this scene (John 12:12–19) participating in various ways in bringing this glory closer?

4. The Jewish leaders are good at making statements that ring with truth to which they are totally oblivious! How is this the case in John 12:19? (Recall John 3:16–17.)

5. Read ahead to John 12:20–23. How do these verses perfectly follow John 12:19? Consider this incident of people from other (non-Jewish) nations of the world coming to Jesus. Why might this incident well provide for Jesus a sort of signal, it seems, that the time for glory has arrived?

Day Three—The Hour Has Come (John 12:20–30)

1. Jesus may have met with these Greeks (Gentiles), but the point here is their ushering in this particular moment. Consider Jesus' statement in John 12:23.

   a. What can we say about this "hour" he mentions, when we see this verse along with John 2:4, 7:30, and 8:20?

   b. Jesus has often referred to himself as the "Son of Man"—sometimes emphasizing his kingly rule and coming judgment (recall Dan. 7:13–14), and sometimes emphasizing his humanity. How does this title seem appropriate here?

   c. *Glorified* refers not just to his resurrection and ascension but first to his death on the cross. How does glory shine in such a death? If glory is shining forth from God's very being, how does that happen on the cross? Just consider; don't write at this point. We shall see this subject unfold.

2. What does the metaphor in John 12:24 communicate about Jesus' death and his view of his death?

3. Consider John 12:25–26, as Jesus shines the same truth on his followers. What are the various implications (both present and future) for those who would follow Jesus to the cross? To love and to hate one's life are purposefully exaggerated terms used to express what attitudes? In what ways are you learning the meaning of these words at this point in your life?

4. Jesus the Son of God knew what he was about to face. Read John 12:27–30.

   a. What two responses struggle within him? Which prevails, and why? (Recall the parallel struggle in Luke 22:42–44.)

   b. Why should we treasure this insight into Jesus' heart?

   c. Observe everything you can about the interaction of Jesus with his Father in these verses.

d. In what ways might God's confirming voice from heaven benefit others more than Christ himself? How does it benefit even you?

Day Four—Who Has Believed? (John 12:31–43)

1. Read John 12:31–32, where Jesus makes three statements about the impending events.

   a. Jesus has said he came to save, not to judge—as he will in the end. However, in what ways have we already seen him bring judgment, which will culminate in the cross (recall John 3:17–19)? How is the cross the ultimate judgment of sin (see 1 Peter 2:24)?

b. Who is the ruler of this world, and how is he cast out by Jesus' death and resurrection? (See Col. 2:13–15 and 1 Peter 5:8.)

c. John explains verse 32 in verse 33. Recall Jesus' previous statement in John 3:14–15. How might "lifted up" imply more than one level of meaning? (See Isa. 52:13, and see how that verse moves right into Isa. 53.)

2. According to the pattern we've often seen, the crowd doesn't get it. They are looking for a Christ who will conquer and reign forever. (Review Lesson 2, Day Two, question 1.) How do their questions actually get right to the heart of the issue (John 12:34), and how does and

doesn't Jesus' response answer their questions (John 12:35–36)?

3. The end of John 12:36 is a sad statement. Find that key word in John 12:36, the same word that is negated in John 12:37 (and quoted in John 12:38). The explanation lies not just in their willful refusal, but also in the truth of John 12:38–40.

   a. What hard truth are these quotations from Isaiah 6 and Isaiah 53 presenting, along with John's commentary in John 12:39? How is this not just a hard truth but also an enlightening and even comforting truth?

b. What is the amazing claim of John 12:41, given to us to explain how Isaiah's words (in the context of his vision of God's glory in Isaiah 6) can apply directly to Jesus? How can John 1:14 help us grasp this?

4. Having begun to grasp this divine glory manifested to us in Christ, what should we find so distressing about the Pharisees mentioned in John 12:42–43? How does all this help clarify the huge stumbling block of the cross for these Jews?

5. Indeed, Jesus' glory is not what the world sees as glory. How have you witnessed or experienced the tension of loving the glory that comes from man more than the glory that comes from God?

Day Five—Final Public Words (John 12:44–50)

1. The final words of this chapter represent Jesus' final public exhortation; after this, he will teach his disciples privately, in the last hours before the cross. What themes of the book do you find reaffirmed in the strong, beautiful words Jesus "cried out" in John 12:44–50?

2. Analyze Jesus' perspective here. What is he most aware of, motivated by, and looking forward to as he speaks these words? What can we learn from this perspective that can help us follow Jesus to the cross?

3. Review that key verse, John 20:31, by memory. Look back through John 12. How does this chapter deepen our understanding of key words in that key verse?

4. We started this chapter with Mary at the feet of Jesus—where she always seems to be found. Finish by meditating on that picture. Say or write a prayer asking God to let you be consumed with Jesus, with his glory and not the world's, and with shining the light of that glory into the darkness until he comes again.

Notes for Lesson 12

Lesson 13 (John 13:1–30)

Christ Embraces the Cross

Day One—Jesus Knew

John has consistently reminded us of the context of the approaching Passover feast (recall John 11:55; 12:1). We are intensely conscious that Jesus the Lamb of God is about to die to take away the sins of the world. This chapter begins just "before the Feast of the Passover," presenting a Christ who enters this momentous 24-hour period with clear knowledge and intention. We enter with him the scene of the "last supper," shown by parallel passages in the Synoptic Gospels to be the Passover meal shared with his twelve disciples (see Mark 14:12–21 and Luke 22:14–15). Much critical debate has surrounded the exact timing of the Passover in relation to these events.[1] Clearly, this Passover meal occurred on the night Jesus was betrayed, the eve of his trial and crucifixion. John offers his unique narrative of this event, portraying the scene in four acts. In the first

1. D. A. Carson's commentary offers a detailed discussion. See his *Gospel According to John* (Grand Rapids, MI: Wm B. Eerdmans, 1991).

act, Jesus dramatically pictures the meaning of the cross (John 13:1-20). The second act shows them all at table, with Jesus directing another kind of cleansing: the sending out of Judas (John 13:21-30).

The remaining two acts will be introduced in Day Five. For this first day, read through John 13:1-30, looking in this reading to find evidences of Jesus' conscious, authoritative direction of events. Write down your observations and thoughts.

(Continued from previous page)

Day Two—Washing Feet (John 13:1–8)

1. How does John 13:1 reveal Jesus' perspective on his death and his mission (both up to this moment and through the moment of his death)? How might that phrase "loved them to the end" or "to the uttermost" provide a good title for this whole scene?

2. What verb goes with the subject "Jesus" in the sentence of John 13:2–4a? In that whole long sentence, what two invisible, interior processes does John illumine as background for this simple action? What difference does each interior process make to the action about to follow?

3. How much do you seek such perspective on all the simple acts of life? How much are you aware of the battles going on, the spiritual forces at work, and the divine calling and

power of one who lives in relationship with God? How might such a perspective challenge and change you?

4. This foot washing would have been the dirtiest job of the lowliest slave. How does the detailed description in John 13:4–5 help make the scene vivid and meaningful?

5. Through this action Jesus offers a dramatic picture of many truths, the first of which becomes clear in John 13:4–8. What is Jesus showing to Peter and to all the disciples? How does Jesus here "act out" the cross in advance? (See also the description of Jesus in Phil. 2:6–8.)

Day Three—If I Have Washed Your Feet. . . . (John 13:6–17)

Consider the scriptural background of washing, cleansing, and purifying. Many of the temple rites prescribed by Old Testament law concerned the sprinkling of blood of sacrificed animals for purposes of purification. All these sacrifices and rituals pointed to the desperate need for purification from sin. Read of that need in Isaiah 1:15–16; read the promise of Isaiah 1:18; read again the promise's fulfillment prophesied in Isaiah 53:4–6.

1. Peter doesn't get it, and he makes this clear! Examine the interaction in John 13:6–8.

    a. First, how would you describe Peter here?

    b. Remembering that this whole scene focuses on looking forward to the cross, how would you explain Jesus' first response (v. 7), and then his second response (v. 8)?

2. Peter not only gives in to Jesus' insistence; he throws himself headlong toward it! Read John 13:9–10.

   a. In responding to Peter's outburst, what is the main truth Jesus figuratively affirms about the cleansing of our hearts through Jesus' blood shed for us?

   b. Jesus stretches the imagery to insert a related truth about spot-cleaning. (Remember the changeable imagery in John 10?) What is the point of the phrase "except for his feet" in the first sentence of verse 10? How might 1 John 1:7–9 shed light on this?

   c. Despite his reference to Judas, Jesus apparently still washes his feet along with the others (John 13:10–12). What are your thoughts about this fact?

3. Jesus then turns the picture in another direction. In John 13:12–17, what is Jesus' main point, and how does he present it emphatically? Now read Philippians 2:3–8.

4. How does the fact that we have been served by Christ himself connect to our service of others? We shall hear him speak more of this, but write down your thoughts at this point.

5. Describe a time when you witnessed or experienced this kind of humble servanthood among followers of Christ.

Day Four—Night Falls (John 13:18–30)

1. For the third time this scene is interrupted by Judas' troublesome presence. In John 13:18–19 Jesus qualifies his call to humble servanthood by acknowledging an exception. How and why did this exception join this group, according to John 13:18? (See Ps. 41:9.) How does the prior glimpse of Judas in John 12:4–6 help fill out the picture?

2. Throughout this whole scene Jesus is clearly preparing his disciples for what is to come. In John 13:19, what key words evidence Jesus' true aim in this preparation?

3. On the foundation of John 13:19, what chain of connection does Jesus explain in John 13:20? (This may "connect ahead" to John 20:21.) In what ways are we part of this chain?

4. But this first foundational group must be purified, all clean—and so we have the second act in this last supper scene. We have seen the reason Jesus reveals in advance the truth about Judas. Now, in John 13:21–30, how would you describe what you see Jesus doing in relation to Judas? (Recall John 13:18.)

5. What a solemn picture of a man personally rejecting the Lord and seeking his own profit—and at the same time a man chosen to betray Jesus. The decisive moment of Satan entering into Judas is a dark one. After that, how does this section wind down dramatically and effectively, in John 13:28–30? How do you respond? *Note: If this was*

Passover night, Passover having begun at sundown, then the following day would begin the week-long Feast of Unleavened Bread. This may be the feast referred to in verse 29.

Day Five—Looking Back and Ahead

We began by saying John presents four acts in this last supper scene. We have seen two: the foot washing and the sending out of Judas. The third is often called "The Upper Room Discourse" (John 13:31–16:33). The fourth is Jesus' final prayer, John 17. Not until after that prayer do the events of the passion story begin. On this night it is as if time stops after that meal, after Judas is gone, and Jesus prepares his disciples for what is to come.

1. Before moving into the Upper Room Discourse, look back to the foot washing scene at the start of this chapter. Picture this scene one more time, and hear Jesus' words to his disciples. Which words stand out to you? What would you like to take away from this scene?

2. If this foot washing scene offers a dramatic picture of what Jesus will do at the cross, then this scene truly reveals what God is like. How does this scene show us what God is like? (Or, how does the cross reveal God's glory?)

3. Look ahead to read and comment on John 13:31–32, where Jesus begins by focusing on what is just ahead of him, starting with the cross—glory. If the Son is glorified in the cross, how is God glorified in the Son? How does God's very being shine through or become magnified at the cross?

4. What a mercy that God so loved us that he gave us his Son to save us. Recall just who this Christ is, from John 1:1–5. This is the Christ we have seen bending down and washing the disciples' dirty feet. This is the Christ who will speak intimately with his followers and even pray for them before he suffers and dies in their place for their sins. What would you pray in response to this?

Notes for Lesson 13

Lesson 14 (John 13:31–14:31)

The Christ of Comfort

In John 12 we saw Jesus leave public exposure for private communion with his disciples in preparation for the cross. At the close of the previous lesson (after the foot washing and the sending out of Judas), we saw Jesus opening his discourse by pointing to glory—a glory that his disciples don't yet understand (John 13:31–32). As this discourse continues, it should encourage our hearts to see Jesus instructing and comforting the ones he has called—loving them to the end.

Day One—Where Are You Going? (John 13:33–14:4)

1. For Jesus, glory involves first the cross but then the return to his Father. Read Jesus' prior mentions of this in John 7:33–34 and 8:21. How do these compare and contrast with John 13:33, 36?

2. In John 13:34–35 Jesus moves on to a theme he will develop further.

   a. How does this theme connect with the foot-washing scene we have just witnessed?

   b. How is this commandment both *not* new and new? See Leviticus 19:18 for the first part, and for the second, consider how Jesus brings a new level of meaning to this command. (Keep this in mind as Jesus continues this discourse.)

   c. In what will this love result? How have you seen this to be true?

3. Jesus lost Peter with his mention of going away! What is good and what is not good in Peter's words (John 13:36–38)? How would you describe Jesus' words as he deals with Peter?

4. What is beautiful (and slightly ironic) about what Jesus begins to do in John 14:1? Find this word *troubled* in John 12:27 and 13:21.

5. Read and meditate on John 14:1–4. In what ways is Jesus encouraging his disciples concerning his imminent departure from them? What exhortation and what command does he give them to help them receive this encouragement? *Note: We might picture these much-discussed*

rooms or "dwelling places" as perhaps even whole apartments within one huge house—enough for a huge extended family!

6. In light of John 14:1–4, read Revelation 21:3. How does this glimpse into the ultimate heart and plan of God lift up your eyes and your heart?

Day Two—Believe Me (John 14:5–14)

1. This chapter brings a series of questions from disciples struggling to understand. Thomas' forthright question brings the sixth of seven "I am" statements (John 14:5–7). Take time to fill in the chart.

   a. What have we learned in this book about Jesus' connection with the Father that explains the claims of John 14:6–7? (See, for example, John 1:1–2; 5:19–24.)

b. Thomas asked only about the way. Why does Jesus include the *way*, the *truth*, and the *life* in his answer?

c. For each of those three words, what does it mean that Jesus *is* this, as opposed to being able to tell about this? Recall the last such statement in John 11:25; how does Thomas need to learn something similar to what Martha needed to learn?

d. How do you respond to Jesus' claim that he is not *a* way but *the* way? Why is this claim such a stumbling block for so many people?

2. Philip is next. He shows that he also has not yet *known* Jesus fully, as he must and will. Read John 14:7–11.

   a. How and why might you and most people identify with Philip's request?

   b. In what ways does Jesus explain his answer to Philip's request? (Note the repeated "in" statements; what is Jesus communicating?)

   c. What does Jesus tell Philip to do? How does this word (repeated three times) hold the key to what Philip is after (recall John 20:31)?

d. How does John 1:18 sum up Philip's problem and the answer to it?

3. That word *believes* is the key to Jesus' resumed teaching in John 14:12–14.

   a. In what possible sense might a believer in Jesus do greater works than he did? How do these works depend on Jesus "going to the Father"? (Subsequent verses will aid in this question, but start by considering what happens in the book of Acts.)

   b. How will a believer accomplish these works, and what will be the purpose of them?

c. What repeated phrase defines this asking? What have we learned about this phrase, starting in the book's prologue? What are the implications here for our prayers?

Day Three—Another Helper (John 14:15–26)

1. Jesus' discourse now turns to the promised Holy Spirit. First, note that this promise comes in the context of a relationship of love between believers and the triune God. What phrases in John 14:15–24 explain how the believer shows (or disproves) his love for God? Why is this context of love so crucial here?

2. Study Jesus' promise of the indwelling Holy Spirit to his disciples—a promise to be fulfilled at Pentecost, after Jesus' death, resurrection, and ascension. The Holy Spirit as the third person of the Trinity has been always active in the world, but after Jesus' death, resurrection, and ascension, the Spirit indwells believers with the truth and power of the risen Christ. Christ, back in heaven with his Father, will ask his Father to send *another* Helper, one like Jesus who was first sent. What observations can you make about this Helper, in John 14:16–17? *Note: "Helper" translates the Greek* parakletos, *which means one called alongside to help, as in a legal advocate. See 1 John 2:1 for the same word applied to Jesus as our "advocate."*

3. Perhaps this promise of the Spirit seems abstract to his bewildered disciples. Jesus promises not only that long-term Helper, but in John 14:18–21, he appears to focus on his brief return to his disciples after the resurrection. This will be the turning point for their understanding. What benefits will be realized after that point? What

is the amazing nature of the relationship of the believer with the Father and the risen Son?

4. Another disciple, Judas (not Iscariot), doesn't get it—asking, in effect, "Only *we* will get to see you?" (John 14:22). Instead of answering directly, Jesus seems to say, "Just believe what I'm telling you," and he returns to the more long-term promise of the indwelling Holy Spirit.

   a. Whose presence will the Holy Spirit bring to dwell in the believer, according to John 14:23–26? Note here the active work of the triune God in the life of a believer. *Note: As Jesus goes to prepare those "rooms," in John 14:1, so God lets us taste in advance that "home" (same word) in John 14:23.*

b. Why is the promise of John 14:25–26 so crucial for this little band of disciples? How are we even now benefiting from this fulfilled promise?

Day Four—Peace (John 14:27–31)

1. Jesus again at this point comforts his disciples, promising them peace (John 14:27). Muse and comment on this verse, considering questions such as the following: What kind of peace is this? How is it different from what the world gives? How does it relate to what Jesus is about to accomplish in his death and resurrection? How does it relate to the promise of the Holy Spirit?

2. Jesus tells his disciples not to be troubled or afraid. What is the source of their trouble and fear here? Have you experienced this kind of fear? How does John 14:27 speak to your troubled or fearful heart?

3. In John 14:28–29 Jesus challenges them to see from a perspective of love and belief—which they will do only later. Why should they rejoice, and how is the Father "greater than" Jesus if they are the same in essence (John 1:1)? (Recall again John 5:19, 30 and Phil. 2:5–11.)

4. Jesus, as we have seen, is aware of Satan at work.

   a. What can Jesus assert about "the ruler of this world," and why, according to John 14:30–31?

b. On what mission and goal is Jesus focused? How does this combination of obedience and love reflect what he has just been teaching the disciples?

The final words of John 14 have been much argued over, as this scene's words are clearly not concluded! Did they leave and continue talking as they walked? Did they speak of leaving and then linger, as groups around a dinner table often do? Look ahead to John 18:1 for the conclusion of all these words.

Day Five—Looking Back

1. Look back through John 14 from the perspective of these struggling disciples. What must it have been like to sit with Jesus and hear him saying these things? In what ways are we today much better off than these disciples at this point, privileged as they were?

2. Look back through John 14 and imagine Jesus' perspective on his disciples. What did he know—about Peter, for example (John 13:38)? How does his perspective reach into layer upon layer of the future?

3. Reread this chapter's promises concerning the Holy Spirit, who is invisible and unknown by unbelievers and yet so real in the lives of believers. Read also Romans 8:9–17. How do you respond?

4. Look back through the chapter in light of John 20:31. How does John 14 show John's aim in his gospel to be at the heart of Jesus' aim in this scene?

Notes for Lesson 14

Initial Observations—Lesson 15

Lesson 15 (John 15–16)

Abiding in Christ

Jesus' final teaching continues to prepare his disciples both for the events about to happen (his death, resurrection, and ascension), and also for the age about to begin: the period between his ascension and his coming again. We live in this period, these "last days" when the Spirit is at work growing the church all over the world, until that day when Jesus will come again in all his glory. How beautiful to see Jesus lovingly ushering his disciples into all these mysteries so that they could later share these mysteries with the world. *Note: This second section of the Upper Room Discourse is "meaty," with themes winding throughout it. The lesson could be divided into two, but you can do it in one!*

Day One—Vine and Branches (John 15:1–16)

1. Read John 15:1–8 and complete the chart of "I Am" Statements. To begin to process this metaphor, consider how Jesus' calling himself "the true vine" fulfills a whole pattern of Old Testament imagery. See, for example, Psalm 80:8–18 (in which the vine is a picture of Israel as God's son who failed) and Isaiah 5:1–7.

2. Jesus was the true Son who did not fail—the true vine. This metaphor winds around like a vine as it develops. Let's begin in John 15:9–10, where Jesus somewhat explains it. Make a sketch of the two-part flow of love in verse 9 and the two-part flow of obedience in verse 10. What are these verses telling us about the process of *abiding*?

3. Now reread and meditate on the picture of abiding, in John 15:1–8. Refer to specific phrases in your answers.

    a. In what ways would you describe the connections portrayed through this vine and branches?

b. How are Jesus' *words* crucial to the connection?

c. How might you sum up what it means to *abide* in him? (Recall also John 6:56.)

d. How do these verses illustrate the truth of the previous "I am"—in John 14:6?

4. This passage is not about trying to stay connected to the vine; it's about what happens if you're connected or not connected, which brings us to *fruit*.

a. The fruit of abiding is scattered throughout this passage like fruit on a vine. In John 15:1–8, 16, what observations can you make concerning this fruit? *Note: Be sure to notice how the process of bearing fruit is initiated, in John 15:16.*

b. In what ways does this passage recall the events of John 13, particularly in relation to Judas, who might offer an example of one *not* abiding and bearing fruit?

5. Jesus' commandment is summed up in John 15:12–14. How does being connected to the true vine let us understand and obey this command? (See also John 13:15, 34.)

6. Read this whole passage one more time, looking for the *benefits* of being connected so intimately to God through Jesus. What various benefits do you find, in John 15:1–16? If we're connected to the vine, how will we view (and not view) these benefits?

Day Two—Hated by the World (John 15:17–16:4)

1. Read back through John 15:1–16. How does Jesus' description of the life of a believer challenge you? How much do you view yourself as personally connected with a loving God and his loving family?

2. Read John 15:18–25. How does John 15:17 both wrap up the previous section and transition into this one?

3. Being in Christ determines our relation not only to God and to fellow believers but to everything else as well.

    a. What things have changed for these disciples in their relation to the world (John 15:18–21)? (See Lesson 4, Day Three, question 2.)

    b. Even with such hard warnings, how are these words of Jesus comforting?

4. According to John 15:21–24, in what ways has Jesus' coming affected those who reject him? (Recall John 9:39–41.)

5. Read John 15:25 with Psalm 69:4. How does not only the quotation from David but also the very insertion of an Old Testament text drive home the guilt of "his own people" who "did not receive him"?

6. Jesus offers two predictions in the next verses. First, when he is gone the witness to him will continue, through both the Holy Spirit and the disciples—which means the world's opposition will also continue (John 15:26–27). (We'll return to the Holy Spirit.) Second, in John 16:1–4, Jesus offers dire predictions about persecution from religious leaders. What reasons does Jesus give here for

offering all these warnings and predictions? How might these reasons be stated using the vine imagery?

DAY THREE—HE WILL GLORIFY ME (JOHN 16:4B–15)

1. Review Jesus' comments concerning the world's opposition (John 15:18–16:4). The disciples experienced this opposition directly as they went on to build the church, but all of Jesus' followers, including us, experience some such opposition. What are the implications here for us? As you write, consider questions such as the following: How have you seen or experienced this in our world today? How can Jesus' words encourage us even now? What do these words imply for us as we teach the next generation?

2. Jesus again mentions his departure in John 16:4b–6, and he makes a statement that seems to contradict John 13:36 and 14:5. Perhaps Jesus knows the disciples are really wondering not so much about where he is going as about why he would leave them, or how they could bear it. Perhaps he means they are not asking this question at this particular moment. In any case, he continues to tell them they will be better off because his going means the Helper's coming. How do the following Old Testament passages look forward to this Spirit-filled age? See Isaiah 44:1–5; Ezekiel 36:24–27; Joel 2:28–29.

3. Note *how* this third person of the Trinity is said to come, according to John 14:16, 14:26, 15:26, and 16:7. What is the role that the Spirit plays in relation to Jesus, according to John 14:26, 15:26, and 16:13–15?

4. Consider the importance of the fact that the persons of the Trinity do not work independently of each other but rather in a mystic unity far beyond our understanding—of one essence, and yet with the Son subordinate to the Father and the Spirit subordinate to Jesus and the Father. Why is it especially important for us today to know that the Spirit's role is to glorify Jesus and the truth of Jesus?

5. Why is it appropriate, considering the Spirit's role in relation to Jesus, that he be called the "Spirit of truth" (John 14:17; 15:26; 16:13)? What does this imply regarding phrases such as "all the truth" and "the things that are to come" (John 16:13)?

6. The Spirit will continue Jesus' conviction of a sinful world, leading some to repentance. Read John 16:8–11, and examine each of the three areas the Spirit

exposes to the truth—all in relation to who Jesus is and what he has done.

Day Four—Sorrow to Joy (John 16:16–24)

1. The disciples' response in John 16:16–18 confirms Jesus' words in John 16:12. What is the huge, looming truth they cannot begin to entertain? How does the promise in John 14:26 and 16:13–14 loom hopefully over this whole passage?

2. In John 16:16–22 Jesus speaks most directly of the time between his death and his resurrection. At his death what will be the opposite reactions of the disciples and the

world? How does Jesus vividly portray the transformation of the disciples' reaction after "a little while"?

3. Muse on John 16:22. What is the nature of this joy? Why will no one be able to take it from them—or us?

4. "In that day" refers to the period of time beginning after the resurrection and continuing now. Why have the disciples until that point asked nothing "in Jesus' name"? What do these words mean for our prayers now (John 16:23–24)? (Recall John 14:12–14; 15:7–8, 16.)

5. How do you think asking and receiving in Jesus' name brings full joy (John 16:24)? In what ways have you witnessed or experienced this kind of joy? How might you live more fully in the joy Jesus is talking about here?

Day Five—Take Heart (John 16:25–33)

1. In John 16:25–28 Jesus acknowledges that he has offered truth through many pictures and "figures of speech."
    a. List some of the many metaphors we have encountered in this book, and consider what role these pictures played for people who heard them from Jesus' lips, before the cross and resurrection.

b. How do these verses promise a new and direct line of communication to God after Jesus' death and resurrection—a curtain torn open?

2. Read John 15:9 with John 16:27 and comment. What is accomplished by Jesus' death and resurrection and ascension?

3. That last question must lead us back to the whole aim of the book. How does John 16:27 help explain the truth of John 20:31?

4. But the disciples still have a way to go in believing. What do they understand, and not understand, in John 16:29–32?

5. Read John 16:32. What does the desertion of even his closest disciples emphasize? What does Jesus' security in his aloneness emphasize?

6. Jesus leaves his disciples "in" which two places in John 16:33? What is the difference? What is the hope here, in these last words to them? How do these words apply to you?

Notes for Lesson 15

Lesson 16 (John 17)

Christ's High-Priestly Prayer

Day One—Overview

How amazing to hear the very words of Jesus Christ, just before he goes to the cross, speaking in prayer to his Father. Spend this first day reading through John 17. As you read, note the way this prayer pulls together many of the themes we have seen throughout the Upper Room Discourse.

Day Two—Jesus Prays for Himself (John 17:1–5)

1. John 17:1 clearly concludes the discourse, with the climax of events imminent. How does the word *hour* here ring like a bell, after all the previous uses of this word? See,

for example, John 2:4; 7:30; 8:20; 12:23. What is the effect of these repeated mentions of time?

2. Note the word, repeated often in John 17:1–5 (and seen often before, especially as the hour has approached), that represents Jesus' main request of his Father at this moment. To *glorify* involves magnifying or showing magnificence. The first place of glorification to which Jesus looks forward is the cross—so certain a prospect that he speaks of it partly as a past event. According to John 17:1–4, how does Jesus aim both to be glorified and to glorify the Father in what he has come to accomplish on earth?

3. In John 17:5, Jesus also looks forward to and asks God for what glory to follow? What can you note about that glory, and what does it reveal about Jesus?

4. Verse 2 explains verse 1, and verse 3 explains verse 2.

   a. Jesus glorifies his Father in carrying out his God-given authoritative saving role. What does this authority involve, according to John 17:2? (Recall Jesus' words concerning this authority to grant life—for example, in John 5:21–24.)

   b. Jesus defines eternal life in John 17:3. It is not an abstract concept. What is it? Comment on this definition, considering questions such as what kind of *knowing* this is, when this knowing begins, and how the two parts of this definition must go together.

Day Three—Jesus Prays for His Disciples (John 17:6–19)

1. In John 17:6–10 Jesus lifts up his disciples before the Father. In these verses how does Jesus repeatedly show the connection of these disciples (and all believers) to the Father, through himself? In what ways have these disciples lived out the definition of verse 3?

2. In the first portion of this prayer how has Jesus affirmed both God's sovereign choosing of his people and the need for people to respond to him (John 17:1–10)? (Look ahead to John 17:12, where we recognize the same truths in reference to Judas, called here the "son of destruction.")

3. Jesus goes on to make petitions for his disciples, whom he is about to leave in the world. We might use the repeated phrase "Keep them in your name" to summarize the petitions in John 17:11–16. What does this phrase mean? From these verses, what specific answers could you give to that question?

4. The next petition is that the disciples be sanctified, which means *set apart as holy* (John 17:17–19).

   a. By what *means* will they be sanctified, according to John 17:17? How does this work? How have we seen it work in Jesus' ministry?

   b. For what *mission* will they be sanctified, according to John 17:18? From what you've observed of Jesus, how might you explain this mission? (Look ahead to John 17:20.)

   c. Through whose *action* will they be sanctified? (The sinless Jesus does not need to be made holy, but consider how he is set apart by God as a holy sacrifice, in order to make us holy.)

Day Four—Jesus Prays for All Believers (John 17:20–26)

1. Jesus' prayer expands to all who will believe, which means he prays for *us*. What is his main request? How might the world interpret this request? How does Jesus explain it in John 17:20–23?

2. Muse on (and perhaps even try diagramming) this picture of unity here, with the flow (of what things?) in all directions among Father, Son, and us. How do you respond?

3. The unity of believers, which is part of the very unity of the Father and Son, is for what purpose in the world,

according to John 17:20–23? How will this unity help accomplish the mission of John 17:20?

4. Jesus' prayer for believers reaches out far, in John 17:24. Write your thoughts on this rich verse, considering questions such as the following: What is Jesus asking here? How does this verse expose the Lord's very heart toward us? How does this verse continue to entwine us in the middle of the love between Father and Son? Where does this verse set our eyes and our hope?

5. How do the chapter's final two verses express the mission of Jesus as we have seen it in this book? How does

the close of Jesus' prayer point ahead to the continuation of the mission?

Day Five—Thinking Back and Ahead

1. How might Jesus' prayer for the Son's and the Father's glory affect our experience of the passion narrative, as we go on to read it?

2. How might Jesus' prayer for his disciples to be *kept* (in him, and from evil, and for joy!) both comfort and alert us believers?

3. How might Jesus' prayer reawaken our sense of mission in the world? How might this prayer readjust your focus on your life's mission? How might it readjust your focus on the church's mission?

4. What implications does this prayer have for your interactions with fellow believers, the body of Christ on earth?

5. Finally, turn your thoughts heavenward, as Jesus did in this prayer. Look to him there, as pictured in John 1:18; 17:5, 24; Colossians 3:1–4; Hebrews 7:25; 10:12–14.

Notes for Lesson 16

Initial Observations—Lesson 17

Lesson 17 (John 18)

Christ Despised and Rejected

Day One—Overview

During the intimacy of Jesus' communion with his disciples in John 13–17, the outward action paused, while Jesus strengthened and prepared them. Now the climactic action toward which the whole book has been moving finally begins, in John 18. Read through the chapter, dividing it into logical sections and writing down your initial thoughts and observations.

Day Two—In the Garden (John 18:1–11)

1. Jesus initiates the action by heading for a place he knows Judas knows—just outside of Jerusalem to the east, probably the Garden of Gethsemane. Look throughout this section for the ways John communicates Jesus' divine direction, his voluntary and sovereign action,

even in these events where he might seem only a victim (John 18:1–11).

2. John does not include Jesus' prayer in the garden but pushes the action right ahead. How do the details in John 18:3 quickly and vividly set the scene? *Note: The "band of soldiers" would be Roman. Consider the array of enemies rising up out of the dark. Who is against Jesus?*

3. Consider the threefold statement of "I am" (literally), in John 18:4–8. (Review Lesson 7, Day Two, question 1 and Lesson 8, Day Five, question 3.) What is happening here with Jesus' words and the response to them?

4. Read John 18:8–9 along with John 6:39; 10:28; 17:12. What is the wonderful truth about Jesus here? How do you respond?

5. John 18:10–11 tells of Peter's famous and typically impetuous action. Of what previous scene does this remind you? The action precipitates a rebuke and some words that clearly reveal Jesus' purpose throughout these scenes.

    a. What does God's cup symbolize in Psalm 75:8; Isaiah 51:17; Jeremiah 25:15–29?

b. What can we understand about Jesus' death on the cross when we understand him to be drinking this cup for us? (See Rom. 1:18; 5:8–9.)

c. What is Jesus' perspective on drinking this cup, in John 18:11? (See also Matt. 26:39, 42.)

d. How should we respond? What response do you find in Psalm 116:12–14?

Day Three—To the High Priest (John 18:12–27)

1. If Scene One was "The Arrest in the Garden," how might you title Scene Two (John 18:12–27)? Read through and make a simple outline of these verses. Why do you think John arranged them this way?

2. Although Caiaphas was the official high priest, Annas had previously been high priest and still retained much authority and respect. How is the whole narrative affected by John's reminder concerning Caiaphas' comment, in John 18:14? (See John 11:49–52, and review Lesson 11, Day Five, questions 1 and 2.)

3. Review John 13:36–38. Then read John 18:15–18, and comment on details and phrases that stand out. *Note: Many have guessed that the other disciple here is John.*

4. In John 18:19–24 the high priest (Annas here) proceeds to question Jesus. However, in what ways does John show it to be the other way around? Jesus is bound and struck, but what is he doing?

5. The story moves back to Peter in John 18:25–27. Contrast him (his position, his words) with Jesus in these alternating scenes. What is the effect? What does it feel like to leave Peter there, in verse 27?

Day Four—Suffered under Pontius Pilate (John 18:28–38)

The morning brings a scene shift—from the Jewish to the Roman authorities. It is the beginning of a whole week of Passover feasting.

1. Even though such laws were sometimes ignored, the Romans passed laws giving themselves the exclusive right to impose the death sentence. Again John steps in and comments. What's the point, in John 18:28–32? (See also John 12:32–33.)

2. Earlier, the Jewish high priest asked about Jesus' "disciples and his teaching." Now, in John 18:33–35, why is Pilate interested in Jesus as *king*? Why do you think Jesus presses him for his motives?

3. In John 18:36–37 Jesus talks about his kingship. What can you observe about his kingship from these verses? Write some thoughts on how Jesus has shown us what it means that his kingdom is not of this world.

4. The Jews had been waiting for a promised king! See John 1:49, and look back to Psalm 132:11–18; Isaiah 9:6–7; Zephaniah 3:14–17. How do these verses shed light on what Jesus is saying here?

5. The king speaks truth, and the ones who belong to his kingdom will hear and obey his word. This scene before Pilate offers a striking example of the way John has shaped his book so that all the themes come together to point to Jesus. Consider these mentions of "truth" and "my voice" (John 18:37–38a) in light of such verses

as John 1:1; 10:3–4; 14:6; 17:17. Do other verses come to mind? What do you see?

Day Five—No Guilt in Him (John 18:38–40)

1. Consider Pilate's verdict in John 18:38b (which will be stated three times in a pattern we can't miss). How is the lamb that is led to the slaughter described in Isaiah 53:9, 11? How is he described later, by Peter, in 1 Peter 1:19? Why is the truth of this verdict so important?

2. With his next question Pilate is perhaps mocking the Jews and Jesus simultaneously. What great ironies do

you find in the chapter's last verses (John 18:38–40)? *Note: Barabbas means, literally, "son of the father."*

3. Take one encouraging look ahead at Peter—after he had seen the risen Christ, after he had begun to know the guidance of the Holy Spirit in making all Jesus' teachings clear to him, after he had begun to preach the Word to others. Peter actually looks back and describes the events we are studying as he speaks to a crowd of Jews in the temple square after healing a lame man. As you read Acts 3:11–19 notice the words, phrases, and concepts showing that Peter (and Jesus' followers) did indeed learn the truth of Jesus' words and works, as we have seen them in John. (See also the prayer in Acts 4:27–28.)

4. Review by memory John 20:31. As you watch Jesus embrace the cross, how is the book's aim being clarified and accomplished in you? Conclude with prayer that you and those studying with you might see and love Jesus the Christ, the Son of God, more clearly and deeply.

Notes for Lesson 17

Initial Observations—Lesson 18

Lesson 18 (John 19)

Christ Crucified, Dead, and Buried

Day One—Overview

In John 19 the story moves inexorably to the cross, to which Jesus has been pointing all along. Spend some moments recalling scenes and words that have consistently pointed us in this direction. Then prayerfully read through this chapter, noting words and phrases that stand out to you and writing your initial thoughts and observations. May this week's study of the Word let us see even more clearly what happened on that cross.

Day Two—Behold the Man (John 19:1–16)

1. John 18 closed in the midst of the scene with Pilate, in which the Roman governor probed Jesus' claim to kingship. The theme of Jesus the King continues to grow and define what happens. Read John 19:1–5; picture each action in order, and picture Jesus after each action. What

is the effect, from Pilate's and the soldiers' point of view? Contrast this with the narrator's omniscient point of view. (What do they mean by "Behold the man!"—and what would John have us understand?)

2. Consider the *Jews*, in particular, in the next verses (John 19:6–16).

   a. Examine their motives and methods, asking why they say what they say at each point.

   b. How do their words echo in light of who they are as God's chosen people, and how has the whole book prepared us for this climactic point?

3. Now consider *Pilate.*

   a. We have seen a flippant and mocking Pilate, but now we see him afraid. Why does Pilate fear, in John 19:7–9? (See also Matt. 27:19.)

   b. Consider the subject of *authority*, which Pilate asserts for himself in the presence of this King (John 19:10). What authority does Pilate actually fear, according to John 19:12–16? Look at him there, mocking, sitting on his judgment seat before Jesus. What is wrong with this picture? (Recall John 5:22–24.)

   c. Note again Pilate's threefold statement of Jesus' innocence. How ironic, in the midst of all these ironies, that this man who mocks truth speaks truth!

Explain one more time the importance of this truth, by stating it in terms of Exodus 12:5.

4. And now consider *Jesus*, surrounded here by those who despise and reject him. How can we not go back to Isaiah 52:13–53:8? Read these verses along with John 19:1–16, commenting on ways in which Jesus' agonies were clearly foretold.

5. Why do you think Jesus gives no answer to Pilate in John 19:9? When he does answer in verse 11, what is his point? Why might the Jewish high priest who handed Jesus over to Pilate have "greater sin" than Pilate, even though they both were guilty of the sin of rejecting Jesus?

Day Three—"Lifted Up Was He To Die" (John 19:16–27)

1. Comment on the setting and scene of the crucifixion, in John 19:16–18. Note that he "went out"—to a hill called Golgotha, outside the city (see Lev. 24:14, 23; Heb. 13:11–13). See also Matthew 27:38.

2. In John 19:19–22 observe the details surrounding Pilate's inscription (a common practice to display a criminal's crimes). How are the results and the responses significant? John doesn't comment on this inscription, but if he had, what might he have said?

3. John does comment in the next verses. Read John 19:23–24 along with Psalm 22:1–18. What connections do you see? What is the general point John would have us grasp?

4. Write your thoughts about the next scene (John 19:25–27), considering questions such as the following: Why did John connect that horrible scene with the soldiers to this one? Why did John include this scene? Besides his mother, these women have not yet appeared in John's gospel. What is the effect of their showing up here? We shall come to know Mary Magdalene better in the next chapter. For now, though, what does this scene show about Jesus?

5. Look back prayerfully through today's verses. Remind yourself of parts of the story John did not include, such as Matthew 27:32–34 and Luke 23:26–31. Finish this day by thinking on the way John has emphasized Jesus' clear mission to obey his Father through his death—thereby bringing life.

DAY FOUR—" '*IT IS FINISHED*!' WAS HIS CRY" (JOHN 19:28–37)

1. Read John 19:28 with John 18:4; how is this pair of "bookends" significant? Think about what Jesus was *knowing* in John 19:28. The same Greek verb appears in four places: twice in John 19:28 (*finished* and *fulfilled*); once in John 19:30 (*finished*); once in John 17:4 (*accomplished*). What does Jesus know and say is finished, in John 19:28–30? (See also Ps. 69:21.)

2. In light of what we've seen of Jesus, and in light of John 10:17–18, how should we describe that moment when Jesus "bowed his head and gave up his spirit" (John 19:30)?

3. In John 19:14, 31, 42, John repeatedly mentions that this is "the day of Preparation"—probably preparation for the Sabbath of Passover week. Jewish law forbade dead bodies of hanged criminals to remain overnight (see Deut. 21:22–23)—and this overnight brought the most special "high day" Sabbath of Passover, beginning at sundown when all work had to end. Read the account in John 19:31–37, along with the description of the Passover lamb in Exodus 12:46, David's prophetic words in Psalm 34:20, and God's words through his prophet in Zechariah 12:10. Now consider two questions concerning John 19:31–37:

    a. What things does John want to make clear at this point in his narrative?

    b. What is he ultimately after here, and why does that not surprise you?

4. Look back over the account of the crucifixion we have just read (John 19:16–37). How does John's goal, fully expressed in John 20:31, affect the way he shapes his account?

Day Five—Courage and Thankfulness (John 19:38–42)

1. What a comfort to come on these two men in the text at this point, men who refuse to hide but instead perform a courageous act for the sake of Jesus. First, write a summary portrait of Joseph of Arimathea, using John 19:38; Matthew 27:57–60; Mark 15:42–46; Luke 23:50–53. What stands out about this man? (See also Isa. 53:9, which has been seen as a prophetic glimpse of Joseph of Arimathea.)

2. Consider Nicodemus and all that John says about him in John 19:39. Connecting the two parts of Nicodemus' story, what might you conclude has happened to him?

3. For what reasons must it have taken courage to ask Pilate for Jesus' body? (See John 12:42–43 to remember what they have overcome.)

4. Between John 19 and 20 lie a night, a whole Sabbath day, and another night. Before looking ahead, let's look back. How can we express the darkness and yet the glory of what happened on the cross? Think back through the book of John to find various ways to say what happened there at Calvary. For example, going back to the prologue, we might say, "Now we have seen his glory, the full extent of it, full of grace and truth." From chapter 1, we might say, "The Lamb of God has been sacrificed for the sin of the world!" Or we might say, "Now we have

seen Jesus stretched out as a ladder opening heaven to us." What might you say, looking back through John, as you meditate on the cross of Jesus?

5. Jesus drank that cup for us. It is finished. Conclude this lesson by spending some moments thanking God for the work of his Son for us on that hill outside Jerusalem. If we need thankful hearts, what better solution than to go back to the cross. Thank him for what you wrote for the previous question. Thank him even before next week's lesson that the story did not end at the cross but was gloriously completed on the third day after Joseph and Nicodemus laid him in that tomb.

Notes for Lesson 18

Lesson 19 (John 20)

Believing in the Christ

Christ's work of suffering the wrath of God in our place on the cross was finished, but the gospel story was not. John ushers us straight ahead to meet the risen Lord Jesus Christ and believe in him, along with the men and women in this chapter.

Day One—He Saw and Believed (John 20:1–10)

1. Mary Magdalene . . . what a beautiful part of the story! After reading John 20:1–2, read also Matthew 27:61 and Luke 8:1–3; 23:55–56. (Recall John 19:25). What things can you observe and know about this woman?

2. The focus shifts to Peter and John. Read John 20:3–10 just to take in the flow of the narrative. What do you notice? How does John tell this, and why? (Recall John 19:35—and recall how we started, in John 1:15, 32, 34.)

3. Not surprisingly, Peter enters the tomb first. It is good to see him here, but it is John's mind and heart we get to see as he encounters the truth all the signs pointed to. Look back to the last sign, which opened this second section of the book. Recall what Jesus desired to happen in Martha and others through that sign (John 11:15, 25–27, 45–48). Confronted with what we might call the sign of all signs, what happens in John here, and why did he still need the physical evidence for it to happen?

4. Although John believed in Jesus as the risen Christ, he did not understand what he later came to understand.

   a. After reading John 20:9, look back to John 14:25–26 and 16:12–15. Read also Luke 24:13–27, 44–49. After his resurrection how did Jesus "jump-start" the process that the Holy Spirit would come and richly perform?

   b. Why "must" Jesus rise from the dead, according to Scripture? Review Lesson 3, Day Four, question 4b.

Day Two—I Have Seen the Lord (John 20:11–18)

1. Many have discussed whether Mary originally came alone or accompanied, or left and came back, etc. Let us see first John's clear focus on Mary and her personal encounter with the risen Lord. Study the process of revelation God

gives her in John 20:11–16. What is her consuming focus throughout? Examine and comment on her responses at each stage of the process.

2. Reread John 10:1–5. How does this picture connect to Mary's experience here? Reread Jesus' comments in John 10:7–18. How, in specific ways, do these comments connect to the whole death and resurrection story we have just read?

3. John 20:17 implies a physical response on Mary's part, which would be natural; the body she saw laid in the grave is alive again! Jesus' words to Mary are all about his resurrected body: he's telling Mary it's not gone from them yet, and he's telling the disciples that it will soon be gone—that the whole process he explained in advance is now happening.

   a. What part has his return to the Father played in Jesus' thinking and teaching, according to John 7:33; 13:1; 16:4–5, 28; 17:5, 11?

   b. Observe carefully the way Jesus words this message about his ascension, his return to his Father, in John 20:17. How are those who believe involved in this process? (See also John 14:6–7; 17:20–23.)

c. Have you wished you could see Jesus in the flesh? How does John 20:17 offer encouragement, even as we long to see him?

4. Consider Mary's response, in John 20:18. Recall John 16:19–22. How is the truth taught being lived out here? How have Jesus' words in John 20:17 confirmed that the joy won't be taken away when his physical presence is taken away?

5. Now is a good time to fill in the story a bit with the parallel gospel accounts. Read Matthew 28:1–10; Mark 16:1–11; Luke 24:1–11. What details stand out, especially

in relation to our understanding of Mary Magdalene's witness to the resurrected Lord?

Day Three—They Saw the Lord (John 20:19–23)

1. We have seen how this chapter brings to light all Jesus' teaching leading up to these final events. Just like Mary, the disciples together experience the promised joy of seeing Jesus again, in John 20:19–21a.

    a. Many surmises have been made about Jesus' resurrected body; what can we say for sure according to this passage?

b. Jesus suffered and died, went that day in spirit to his Father, and then on the third day was reunited with his body—resurrected! One thing we can say for sure is that, as believers in him, our bodies will be resurrected as well. Read 1 Corinthians 15:3–58, not to grasp every detail but to get the main ideas and the main hope we have because of Jesus' bodily death *and resurrection*. Why is Jesus' resurrection so crucial, and how should the hope of it lift our hearts?

2. Comment on another promise that Jesus brings to life in his repeated greeting to them (John 20:19, 21; see also John 14:27; 16:33). Why is the reminder of this promise so crucial at this specific time?

3. This peace is not an abstract feeling but rather the experience of a restored relationship with God. To what does this relationship lead, according to John 20:21b? In what

ways is this commission explained by John 13:15–16; 14:12; 15:8–10, 27; 17:18–23?

4. This commission would be too frightening if it weren't for the relationship on which it depends—and the present link to that relationship, the Spirit, who dwells in us until we see Jesus again. John 20:22–23 brings to the forefront this promised indwelling Holy Spirit and the fruit that will come through those indwelled by the Spirit.

   a. Much critical discussion surrounds John 20:22. Merrill Tenney writes, "This was the initial announcement of which Pentecost was the historic fulfillment."[1] D. A. Carson calls it "a kind of acted parable pointing forward to the full enduement still to come."[2] How does this approach make sense, especially in light of Jesus' teaching concerning when and how the Spirit would come, in John 16:7?

1. Merrill C. Tenney, "The Gospel of John," *The Expositor's Bible Commentary* (Grand Rapids, MI: Zondervan, 1981), 9:193.

2. D. A. Carson, *The Gospel according to John* (Grand Rapids, MI: Wm. B. Eerdmans, 1991), 655.

b. The commission involves bringing others to believe through the word Jesus gave to the disciples (see John 17:20). In John 20:23, Jesus addresses the disciples as the first and representative carriers of that gospel word. God himself is the forgiver or non-forgiver of sins, but how do the proclaimers of his word become the ones through whom the Spirit works to that end—for example, in Acts 2:38–41?

5. We just read the end of the story of Pentecost, as Peter finished his sermon on that occasion. Go back and fill in the beginning, in Acts 1:6–11 and 2:1–21. Finish this day's study by simply reading and relishing this fulfillment of Jesus' words.

DAY FOUR—BELIEVE (JOHN 20:24–29)

1. Describe Thomas from what you can see in John 20:24–25. See also John 11:16 and 14:5.

2. Read John 20:24–27; compare Thomas' and Jesus' words. What was Jesus revealing along with his wounds?

3. In what ways does Thomas' affirmation (John 20:28) bring a huge climax to this chapter and this whole book? (As you answer, don't forget to go all the way back to the prologue.)

4. Note that key word moving like a thread through this scene, telling Thomas' story. Consider Jesus' final words to him in John 20:29. How is this kind of believing affirmed earlier in this chapter and throughout the book? (See, for example, John 2:23; 14:11.)

5. Who are those in Jesus' second category—not seeing, yet believing? Why does Jesus declare them blessed? See Peter's view of it in 1 Peter 1:8–9. What is your response to this blessing of Jesus and these words of Peter?

Day Five—So That You May Believe (John 20:30–31)

1. Thomas's affirmation of belief climactically illustrates and ushers in John's conclusion, which tells his reader exactly why he has written the book. How far away these verses seemed at the start—and yet how present they have been throughout. For this final day, write down key words and phrases from this concluding purpose statement. For each, look/think back through the book and comment on how each has been deepened and developed. Note key verses or scenes that come to mind for each.

(Continued from previous page)

2. John's gospel originally was read by both Jews and Gentiles, believing and unbelieving. What aspects of this gospel would especially speak to a Jewish reader? How would John also draw in a Gentile reader? Consider the various ways the book might accomplish its aim in the lives of these different audiences.

3. How can John's gospel, developed in John's unique and beautiful style, speak into many different contexts today? Have you seen it do so? How have you personally experienced John's clear aim accomplished in your own growth and understanding?

Notes for Lesson 19

Lesson 20 (John 21)

Following Christ

The book has been concluded. The final chapter has been called an Epilogue, in which the One sent from God sends us out along with the disciples.

Day One—Come and Have Breakfast (John 21:1–14)

1. Consider how John 21:1–3 establishes great symmetry and completion for this book, not only with persons and place, but also with a final *revealing* of Jesus to us. How did the book start by speaking of Jesus being revealed, and how has the whole book been about that? See also John 21:14.

2. Whether the risen Jesus was difficult to recognize because of tears (recall Mary Magdalene) or a different look to a glorified body or just a misty morning, no one knows. But picture the disciples in the boat after a fruitless night of fishing, and Jesus standing on the shore calling to them. What somewhat similar former scene comes to mind? In John 21:3–8, how do John and Peter both act remarkably like themselves, as we have come to know each of them? What other details of the narrative do you notice?

3. How might a previous similar experience have helped John quickly recognize Jesus (Luke 5:1–11)?

4. We have watched Jesus heal the blind, wash feet, offer water—and so we know this beautiful scene of John 21:9–14 is not without deep meaning. John has not men-

tioned Jesus' calling the disciples to be "fishers of men," so one might doubt this scene's direct connection to that concept. But John *has* shown us scenes of Jesus *feeding* with abundance when it seemed there was none. Look back through John 6. In what ways might this final story connect with that one?

5. Read John 21:9–14 one more time, and imagine yourself in the scene—with sights, smells, sensations, tastes, and sounds. And then consider the disciples' reverent reticence before the Lord Jesus. Think of Thomas's words. What must have been in their hearts in these moments?

Day Two—Feed My Sheep (John 21:15–19)

1. In John, we have often found an explanation attached to a miracle (cf. John 6). So in this last chapter, after Jesus feeds, he talks about feeding. Consider carefully these

three questions and answers. What do you think is going on here (John 21:15–17)? *Note: John often uses synonyms within one passage; here he uses several different Greek words for* love, feed, *and* sheep. *We can probably get the main point without drawing too many distinctions among the words.*

2. Jesus' message in John 6 was that we must feed (*believe*) on Jesus himself as the bread of life sacrificed for us in order to receive eternal life. How did Jesus come (John 1:1), and what did he give us (John 6:68; 17:14), in order that we might believe? What do the sheep hear and follow, in John 10? What would the disciples use to help feed others, so that others might believe (John 14:26; 16:13–14; 17:20)? How beautiful to see Peter in a sense reinstated here—to do what?

3. We already saw Peter preaching the Word at Pentecost! Peter continued to lead the church faithfully according to the gospel he had learned from Jesus himself. (See him speaking, for example, in Acts 15:6–11.) How can we tell he truly heard Jesus in John's final scene, from the words in 1 Peter 5:1–4?

4. In John 21:18–19, Jesus symbolically predicts Peter's death by crucifixion. Peter indeed had been martyred by the time John wrote this gospel.

   a. What words stand out in these verses, and why?

   b. Look back to John 13:36–38, and comment.

5. What encouragement and challenge do you find, personally, in the story of Peter?

Day Three—Last Things (John 21:20–25)

1. Consider a few questions about John 21:20–23:

   a. What does Jesus want to impress upon Peter?

   b. What does John want to clarify for his readers? Why would this be important for the early church to understand?

2. What is the wonderful truth about Jesus lurking in John 21:22–23? How has Jesus shed light on that truth through his words of teaching? See, for example, John 5:25–29; 6:39–40; 14:3.

3. In John 21:24, the disciple whom Jesus loved is identified as the disciple who has written the book.

   a. What is his main concern, and where have we seen this concern before in the last several chapters?

   b. Connect *witness* and *testimony* to the very first chapter of his book.

c. John's "we" may represent just himself, or the group of disciples with whom John followed Jesus, or all who believe that Jesus is the Christ, the Son of God. One more time, how has this book assured us that the words of this writer are to be trusted as true?

4. Consider the book's final verse. In what sense would this supposition be true? How does this ending call back to our thoughts the book's stated aim?

5. In what ways is this whole epilogue effective in offering not an end to thoughts, but food for more?

Day Four—Looking Back

1. We will conclude with several large questions that ask us to look back over this study of the gospel of John. First, consider the role of *Old Testament Scripture* in John's gospel. Page back through your lessons, starting with the very first one, and notice how many times we turned to the Old Testament and why. Which Old Testament passages have most invaded your thoughts? How? What has been John's point with all his scriptural echoes? What has John shown to be Jesus' role in relation to the whole counsel of Scripture?

(Continued from previous page)

(Continued from previous page)

2. Finally, on this next-to-last day, look back through your study once more, this time noting and relishing all the images or pictures that have conveyed the truth of this gospel. Write down what you associate with each. For example, you might note the vine and branches, and then write "intimacy with the Lord, through abiding in his word." Then look at all these pictures together; set up a gallery in your mind. Why do you think Jesus chose to communicate so often in this way? How do these images affect your mind and heart, and ultimately your believing relationship with Jesus the Christ, the Son of God?

(Continued from previous page)

(Continued from previous page)

Day Five—Looking at Him

In conclusion, look back through your study one more time, noting the many occasions when Jesus took the time to give himself with complete focus and attention to one human being. The first such encounter would be with Nathanael, in the first chapter. Of course Jesus often spoke to crowds, but it is amazing to see those occasions interspersed consistently with one-on-one encounters. What do you notice about Jesus in these encounters as you recall them? What amazes you about these encounters? Which ones touch you most, and why? When you have concluded this overview, spend some one-on-one time yourself with your Lord God who loves you like this, personally—so much that for you, personally, Jesus died and rose and is coming again. How can God create and rule the whole universe and still care about you and me? That is the wonder, and that is the mystery of the Word made flesh. Conclude by thanking God with a believing heart for this wonder—for Jesus the Christ, the Son of God, in whose name we have life.

(Continued from previous page)

(Continued from previous page)

Notes for Lesson 20

Notes for Leaders

What a privilege it is to lead a group in studying the Word of God! Following are six principles offered to help guide you as you lead.

1. The Primacy of the Biblical Text

If you forget all the other principles, I encourage you to hold on to this one! The Bible is God speaking to us, through his inspired Word—living and active and sharper than a two-edged sword. As leaders, we aim to point people as effectively as possible into this Word. We can trust the Bible to do all that God intends in the lives of those studying with us.

This means that the job of a leader is to direct the conversation of a group constantly back into the text. If you "get stuck," usually the best thing to say is: "Let's go back to the text and read it again . . . ." The questions in this study aim to lead people into the text, rather than into a swirl of personal opinions about the topics of the text; therefore, depending on the questions should help. Personal opinions and experiences will often enrich your group's interactions; however, many Bible studies these days have moved almost exclusively into the realm of "What does this mean to me?" rather than first trying to get straight on "What does this mean?"

We'll never understand the text perfectly, but we can stand on one of the great principles of the Reformation: the *perspicuity* of Scripture. This simply means *understandability*. God made us word-creatures, in his image, and he gave us a Word that he wants us to understand more and more, with careful reading and study, and shared counsel and prayer.

The primacy of the text implies less of a dependence on commentaries and answer guides than often has been the case. I do not offer answers to the questions, because the answers are in the biblical text, and we desperately need to learn how to dig in and find them. When individuals articulate what they find for themselves (leaders included!), they have learned more, with each of their answers, about studying God's Word. These competencies are then transferable and applicable in every other study of the Bible. Without a set of answers, a leader will not be an "answer person," but rather a fellow searcher of the Scriptures.

Helps *are* helpful in the right place! It is good to keep at hand a Bible dictionary of some kind. The lessons themselves actually offer context and help with the questions as they are asked. A few commentaries are listed in the "Notes on Translations and Study Helps," and these can give further guidance after one has spent good time with the text itself. I place great importance as well on the help of leaders and teachers in one's church, which leads us into the second principle.

2. The Context of the Church

As Christians, we have a new identity: we are part of the body of Christ. According to the New Testament, that body is clearly meant to live and work in local bodies, local churches. The ideal context for Bible study is within a church body—one that is reaching out in all directions to the people around it. (Bible studies can be the best places for evangelism!) I realize that these studies will be used in all kinds of ways and places; but whatever the context, I would hope that the group leaders have a layer of solid church leaders around them, people to whom they can go with questions and concerns as they study the Scriptures. When a leader doesn't know the answer to a question that arises, it's really OK to say, "I don't know. But I'll be happy to try to find out." Then that leader can go to pastors and teachers, as well as to commentaries, to learn more.

The church context has many ramifications for Bible study. For example, when a visitor attends a study and comes to know the Lord, the visitor—and his or her family—can be plugged into the context of the church. For another example, what happens in a Bible study often can be integrated with other courses of study within the church, and even with the preaching, so that the whole body learns and grows together. This depends, of course, on the connection of those leading the study with those leading the church—a connection that I have found to be most fruitful and encouraging.

3. The Importance of Planning and Thinking Ahead

How many of us have experienced the rush to get to Bible study on time . . . or have jumped in without thinking through what will happen during the precious minutes of group interaction . . . or have felt out of control as we've made our way through a quarter of the questions and used up three-quarters of the time!

It is crucial, after having worked through the lesson yourself, to think it through from the perspective of leading the discussion. How will you open the session, giving perhaps a nutshell statement of the main theme and the central goals for the day? (Each lesson offers a brief introduction that will help with the opening.) Which questions do you not want to miss discussing, and which ones could you quickly summarize or even skip? How much time would you like to allot for the different sections of the study?

If you're leading a group by yourself, you will need to prepare extra carefully—and that can be done! If you're part of a larger study, perhaps with multiple small groups, it's helpful for the various group leaders to meet together and to help each other with the planning. Often, a group of leaders meets early on the morning of a study, in order to help the others with the fruit of their study, plan the group time, and pray—which leads into the fourth principle.

4. The Crucial Role of Prayer

If these words we're studying are truly the inspired Word of God, then how much we need to ask for his Spirit's help and guidance as we study his revelation! This is a prayer found often in Scripture itself, and a prayer God evidently loves to answer: that he would give us understanding of his truth, according to his Word. I encourage you as a leader to pray before and as you work through the lesson, to encourage those in your group to do the same, to model this kind of prayer as you lead the group time, to pray for your group members by name throughout the week, and to ask one or two "prayer warriors" in your life to pray for you as you lead.

5. The Sensitive Art of Leading

Whole manuals, of course, have been written on this subject! Actually, the four principles preceding this one may be most fundamental in cultivating your group leadership ability. Again, I encourage you to consider yourself not as a person with all the right answers, but rather as one who studies along with the people in your group—and who then facilitates the group members' discussion of all they have discovered in the Scriptures.

There is always a tension between pouring out the wisdom of all your own preparation and knowledge, on the one hand, and encouraging those in your group to relish and share all they have learned, on the other. I advise leaders to lean more heavily toward the latter, reserving the former to steer gently and wisely through a well-planned group discussion. What we're trying to accomplish is not to cement our own roles as leaders, but to participate in God's work of raising up mature Christians who know how to study and understand the Word—and who will themselves become equipped to lead.

With specific issues in group leading—such as encouraging everybody to talk, or handling one who talks too much—I encourage you to seek the counsel of one with experience in leading groups. There is no better help than the mentoring and prayerful support of a wise person who has been there! That's even better than the best "how-to" manual. If you have a number of group leaders, perhaps you will invite an experienced group leader to come and conduct a practical session on how to lead.

Remember: the default move is, "Back to the text!"

6. The Power of the Scriptures to Delight

Finally, in the midst of it all, let us not forget to delight together in the Scriptures! We should be serious but not joyless! In fact, we as leaders should model for our groups a growing and satisfying delight in the Word of God—as we notice its beauty, stop to linger over a lovely word or phrase, enjoy the poetry, appreciate the shape of a passage from beginning to end, laugh at a touch of irony or an image that hits home, wonder over a truth that pierces the soul.

May we share and spread the response of Jeremiah, who said:

> Your words were found, and I ate them,
> and your words became to me a joy
> and the delight of my heart. (Jer. 15:16)

Outline of John

I. Prologue (John 1:1–18)

II. The Light Is Revealed (John 1:19–10:42)

   A. Spreading Light (John 1:19–4:54)

   B. The Light Shines, Hated by Many (John 5:1–10:42)

III. Seeing His Glory (John 11:1–20:31)

   A. Heading for Glory (John 11:1–12:50)

   B. Preparation for Glory (John 13–17)

   C. The Cross and Resurrection (John 18–20)

IV. Epilogue (John 21)

Seven Signs

Jesus' signs are central to this gospel. John tells us exactly why, in John 20:30–31. Consider, as you chart these signs, just how they help us see and believe in Jesus. The third column you might fill in gradually and perhaps come back to as you see the signs unfold.

Scripture reference	Nature of sign	Observations/comments about the sign

SEVEN "I AM" STATEMENTS

John's prologue tells us who Jesus is, and then Jesus comes on the scene and reveals himself. These statements stand out in the process of revelation. The third column you might fill in gradually and perhaps come back to as you see these statements grow in meaning.

Scripture reference	Statement	Observations/comments about the statement

Jewish Festivals

Jesus worked purposefully through the rhythm of the Jewish feast days established in the Old Testament law. John highlights these festivals to show how Jesus fulfills everything they celebrate. One crucial festival appears three times. The third column you might fill in gradually and perhaps come back to as the Old Testament context becomes increasingly clear.

Scripture reference	Festival	Observations/comments about the festival

Suggested Memory Passages

What an opportunity, as we study the Word, to hide that Word in our hearts. We don't memorize verses or passages from the Bible enough these days. I would like to challenge those of you doing this study to choose one or two substantial passages to commit to memory. When you can't sleep at night, saying one verse sometimes doesn't take long enough to settle your heart and lead you back to rest! I find that saying a longer passage (or sometimes a whole hymn, with all the verses!) does lead my thoughts and my imagination in good paths—and often into the rest of sleep. Memory passages are wonderful to work on while you're walking or exercising. Verses we've hidden in our hearts come into our minds at the most amazing and helpful times, as God uses his Word to accomplish all that he promises in us and through us. Even if you're not great at memorization, words and phrases you've worked on will stick with you and come back to you. The following are suggested longer passages from John; choose one or more of these or others. John is full of wonderful passages to memorize.

- John 1:1–18 (the prologue—which becomes ever richer as you study the whole book)

- John 3:16–20 (Why not put that famous verse in its beautiful context?)
- John 14:1–7 (These verses focus our thoughts on Jesus and, through him, on heaven.)
- John 15:1–11 or 1–17 (Such a fruitful picture to fill your thoughts!)
- John 20:30–31 (Of course!)

Notes on Translations and Study Helps

This study can be done with any reliable translation of the Bible, although I do recommend the English Standard Version for its essentially literal but beautifully readable translation of the original languages. In preparing this study, I have used and quoted from the ESV, published by Crossway Bibles in Wheaton, Illinois.

These lessons are designed to be completed with only the Bible open in front of you. The point is to grapple with the text, not with what others have said about the text. The goal is to know, increasingly, the joy and reward of digging into the Scriptures, God's breathed-out words, which are not only able to make us wise for salvation through faith in Christ Jesus but also profitable for teaching, reproof, correction, and training in righteousness, so that each of us may be competent, equipped for every good work (2 Tim. 3:15–17). To help you "dig in," basic and helpful contexts and comments are given throughout the lessons. I have used and learned from the following books in my own study and preparation; you may find sources such as these helpful at some point.

GENERAL HANDBOOKS:

The Crossway Comprehensive Concordance of the Holy Bible: English Standard Version. Compiled by William D. Mounce. Wheaton: Crossway Books, 2002. (Other concordances are also available, from various publishers and for different translations.)

The Illustrated Bible Dictionary. 4 vols. Wheaton: Tyndale House Publishers, 1980. (*The Zondervan Pictorial Encyclopedia of the Bible* is similarly helpful.)

Ryken, Leland, James Wilhoit, and Tremper Longman III, eds. *Dictionary of Biblical Imagery*. Downers Grove, IL: InterVarsity Press, 1998.

Ryken, Leland, Philip Ryken, and James Wilhoit. *Ryken's Bible Handbook*. Wheaton: Tyndale House Publishers, 2005.

Vine's Complete Expository Dictionary of Old and New Testament Words. Nashville: Thomas Nelson, 1984.

COMMENTARIES:

Boice, James Montgomery. *The Gospel of John*, 5 vols. Grand Rapids, MI: Baker Books, 1999.

Carson, D. A. *The Gospel according to John*. Pillar New Testament Commentary. Grand Rapids, MI: Wm. B. Eerdmans Pub. Co., 1991.

Hughes, R. Kent. *John: That You May Believe*. Wheaton, IL: Crossway Books, 1999.

Read Mark Learn: John. Developed by St. Helen's Church, Bishopsgate. Ross-shire, Scotland: Christian Focus Publications Ltd., 2008.

Lucas, Dick, and William Philip. *Teaching John: Unlocking the Gospel of John for the Bible Teacher*. Ross-shire, Scotland: Christian Focus Publications Ltd., with Proclamation Trust Media, 2008.

Morris, Leon. *The Gospel according to John*. The New International Commentary on the New Testament. Grand Rapids, MI: Wm. B. Eerdmans Pub. Co., 1971.

Tenney, Merrill C. "The Gospel of John." In *The Expositor's Bible Commentary*, vol. 9, pp. 3–203. Grand Rapids, MI: Zondervan Publishing House, 1981.

Study Bible:

ESV Study Bible. English Standard Version. Wheaton, IL: Crossway Bibles, 2008.

Kathleen Nielson (MA, PhD in literature, Vanderbilt University) has taught in the English departments at Vanderbilt University, Bethel College (Minnesota), and Wheaton College. She is the author of numerous Bible studies, the book *Bible Study: Following the Ways of the Word*, and various articles and poems. Kathleen has directed and taught women's Bible studies at several churches and speaks extensively at conferences and retreats. She serves as advisor and editor for The Gospel Coalition and was its director of women's initiatives from 2010–2017. She is also on the board of directors of The Charles Simeon Trust.

Kathleen and her husband Niel have three sons, two beautiful daughters-in-law, and a growing number of grandchildren!